IN THE KNOW

A Swim Parent's Guide

NICK BAKER, FOUNDER OF PEAK PERFORMANCE SWIM CAMP & 1992 OLYMPIC COACH

Positive Swimming
Orlando, Florida

CONTENTS

ABOUT THE AUTHOR

Nick Baker has been involved in the sport of competitive swimming since 1961. He swam competitively for 11 years, coached at the club level for 21 years, and has coached swim camps exclusively for 22 years. Below are some of his career highlights:

1968 — 200 Breaststroke Olympic Trial Qualifier

1972-1993 — Professional Club Coach

1989 — Canada Games Coach

1991 — World Junior Olympic Coach – Madrid, Spain

1992 — Olympic Coach – Barcelona, Spain (Personal Coach of Lisa Flood)

1993-Present — Professional Camp Coach and Private Coach

1996-Present — Founder and Head Coach of Peak Performance Swim Camp Author of Two Popular Swimming-Related Books, *101 Winning Ways* and *The Swimming Triangle* Featured Writer for Swimming World Magazine Featured Clinician at Coaching Clinics Around the World

1996-Present — Director and Head Coach at Over 400 PEAK Swim Camps and Clinics Throughout the United States and 15 Foreign Countries

2014 — More than 1,200 Swimmers, from 40 Countries, Attended Peak Performance Swim Camp

Past 43 years — Coached many Elite-Level Athletes, including World Record Holders, Olympic Medalists, Olympic Finalists, Olympic Trial Qualifiers, NCAA Champions, Senior and Junior National Qualifiers, Zone Champions, State Champions, High School State Champions, Junior Olympic Champions and more

INTRODUCTION

As the parent you are ultimately responsible for the upbringing of your child, but you share that responsibility with others in your inner circle and community. These include family members, friends, babysitters, teachers, tutors, and coaches.

Sharing your child requires a certain degree of trust gained through experience and knowledge. You would never blindly ask a stranger to take responsibility for your child or expose your child to a situation you knew little or nothing about. Yet many parents are naive when it comes to sharing their child with swimming. They know little about what constitutes a good swim coach or swim team, the training and competitive environment, or the necessary steps that must be taken to achieve success.

In The Know — A Swim Parent's Guide contains pearls of wisdom gleaned from coaching "in the trenches" for more than forty years. It sheds bright light on many of the unanswered questions parents have about swimming, and guides them in making the right decisions for their child.

* A portion of the material contained in this book is covered more extensively in my book, *The Swimming Triangle*.

CHAPTER 1.

BROADEN YOUR AWARENESS

The first chapter examines a variety of important swimming related topics that impact the child's swimming. Parents who possess greater knowledge can do more to help their child succeed.

BENEFITS OF SWIMMING

Swimmers give up so much to pursue the sport they love, but they also receive much in return. Mental benefits include increased confidence, focus, and discipline, qualities that advantage the child throughout life.

Physical benefits include improved health, wellness, and fitness, which extend well beyond a child's swimming career. Other benefits include friendships, heightened status amongst peers and public recognition, travel and college scholarship opportunities, and the potential to compete at an elite level one day.

WHAT TO LOOK FOR IN A SWIM TEAM

Deciding on the right swim team can be a real challenge for any parent. To assist in the search, I compiled a list of top considerations:

- Look for a swim team that gets results.

- Look for a swim team that has a clear mission statement.

- Look for a swim team that has a code of conduct for coaches, parents, and swimmers.

- Look for a swim team that is well organized and effective in communicating with parents.

- Look for a swim team with quality training facilities.

- Look for a swim team that offers adequate training hours for all levels of swimmers.

- Look for a swim team that provides quality coaching for all levels of swimmers.

- Look for a swim team with a low coach turnover rate.

- Look for a swim team with a low swimmer-to-coach ratio.

- Look for a swim team that is not overcrowded.

- Look for a swim team that offers comprehensive dry-land training.

- Look for a swim team that develops high-quality swimmers from within the program.

- Look for a swim team with certified coaches.

- Look for a swim team that provides continuing education for coaches.

- Look for a swim team with a low swimmer attrition rate.

- Look for a swim team with an abundant number of swimmers in all age groups.

- Look for a swim team that offers quality competition for all levels of swimmers.

- Look for a swim team with a transparent policy for swimmer placement and advancement.

- Look for a swim team with an upbeat team environment.

- Look for a swim team with a low rate of swimming related injuries.

- Look for a swim team that offers ongoing team building and social activities.

- Look for a swim team that values parental input.

- Look for a swim team with an active parent body.

- Look for a swim team within proximity of home.

HOME GROWN

Back in the 1990's I was an assistant coach at a large swim team. At the time, we were number one in the world. Virtually every top swimmer on the team had been recruited from other teams rather than developed in-house. Parents should exercise caution when choosing a swim team for their child. Does the team have the coaching and structure in place to develop elite-level swimmers from the ground up or do they heavily recruit from other teams? A team that "grows their own" is the absolute best place for your child.

Finding the right swim coach is of primary importance. Parents should move cautiously and consider all the facts. To assist in the search, I compiled a list of top considerations:

- Look for a swim coach who gets results.

- Look for a swim coach who likes to work with swimmers of all ability levels.

- Look for a swim coach who coaches with passion.

- Look for a swim coach who inspires swimmers.

- Look for a swim coach who keeps it fun.

- Look for a swim coach who is certified.

- Look for a swim coach with a well-defined coaching philosophy.

- Look for a swim coach who is organized.

- Look for a swim coach who is open minded.

- Look for a swim coach who makes practices exciting and challenging.

- Look for a swim coach who is proficient in teaching the four competitive strokes.

- Look for a swim coach who offers IM-based training and four stroke training.

- Look for a swim coach who provides both endurance-based and sprint-based training.

- Look for a swim coach who maintains discipline.

- Look for a swim coach who is firm, but fair.

- Look for a swim coach who emphasizes technique.

- Look for a swim coach with admirable character traits.

- Look for a swim coach who puts the well-being of swimmers first.

- Look for a coach who is even-tempered.

- Look for a swim coach who treats swimmers with respect.

- Look for a swim coach who treats staff members with respect.

- Look for a swim coach who is patient.

- Look for a swim coach who spends time with every swimmer in the group.

- Look for a swim coach who communicates with parents.

- Look for a swim coach who stresses academics.

- Look for a swim coach who offers a balanced competitive schedule.

- Look for a swim coach who gives swimmers short breaks to recharge during non-critical periods of the year.

- Look for a swim coach who strives to make swimming a great experience for all.

- Look for a swim coach who recognizes the achievement of all swimmers.

STYLE IS EVERYTHING

A positive coaching style is essential in developing a child's swimming potential. Unfortunately, not all coaches believe in the power of positivity choosing unsavory and antiquated methods of motivation including fear, threats, and intimidation. Treating swimmers in this manner is a form of bullying that diminishes self-worth and swimming performance.

A 2003 study by Dr. Stephan Joseph at the University of Warwick found that verbal abuse can do significant harm to a person's self-worth. A 2005 study at UCLA found that children continually subjected to name calling felt humiliated, anxious, angry, and disliked school to a greater extent. Moreover, a 2007 Penn State study found that children bullied or expecting to be bullied by their teachers experienced increased levels of cortisol commonly known as the stress hormone. Ironically, when cortisol levels spike, the ability to think clearly and remember is significantly compromised.

Ideal coaches are professional through and through and set high standards. While they demand much, they do so in a manner that enhances swimmers' self-worth. Rather than tear swimmers down, they build them up via a positive coaching style.

SWIM PARENT SURVEY

In a perfect world, parents would know if the choices they made regarding their child's swimming were the right ones. To assist in that determination, I created a parent survey. A simple "yes/no response" to each question will give parents a clearer picture of their child's current state of swimming:

- Is your child making visible progress?

- Is your child having fun?

- Does your child like the coach?

- Does your child feel part of the team?

- Has your child made friends on the team?

- Does the team have spirit?

- Does your child look forward to going to practice?

- Can your child legally perform all four strokes?

- Can your child execute a proper front start and back start?

- Can your child legally perform all four turns?

- Does the coach correct your child's mistakes?

- Has your child's fitness improved?

- Does the coach provide adequate competitive opportunities for your child?

- Does your child look forward to competing?

- Does your child compete in a variety of events?

- Is your child dropping times in competition?

- Has your child qualified for higher levels of competition?

- Has your child been disqualified?

- Has the reason for their disqualification been corrected?

- Does the coach ever work individually with your child?

- Is the swimmer-to-coach ratio acceptable?

- Is the quality of coaching acceptable?

- Is the coach a positive role model?

- Does the coach motivate your child?

- Has your child set ambitious swimming goals?

- Is the pool overcrowded?

- Are there lifeguards on duty?

- Are the coaches certified in safety procedures?

- Are the pool conditions (air and water quality) satisfactory?

- Does the coach speak to parents?

- Does the team value your membership?

- Does the team communicate well with parents?

- Does the team perform well in competition?

APPLES ON A TREE

Apples on a tree ripen at different times, some early, some late, and some in between. The same scenario holds true in swimming where swimmers "ripen" at various stages, some as young age groupers, some during puberty, and some in their teenage years. Many parents mistakenly believe that swimmers must ripen by the age of ten to reach the elite level of swimming at a later point. On the contrary, extensive research indicates that the vast majority of swimmers begin the process during puberty or beyond.

THE NUMBERS DO NOT LIE

It is not uncommon for a swimming career to span ten to fourteen years. Most swimmers join a swim team as young age groupers and retire around the age of twenty-two or upon graduating from college. A sport of this duration requires a multi-year approach focused on gradual mental, technical, and physical development with the best interest of swimmers in mind at all times.

Unfortunately, many coaches (and parents) possess an "I want it all, and I want it now mentally". Rather than support a multi-year approach, they choose to fast track swimmers and short-circuit the process. While this approach may work in the short-term, the numbers do not lie. A study conducted by United States Swimming found:

- Only 8.6% of girls ranked in the Top 100 as 11-12 year olds remained in the Top 100 as 17-18 year olds.

- Only 10.9% of boys ranked in the Top 100 as 11-12 year olds remained in the Top 100 as 17-18 year olds.

- Only 15.4% of girls ranked in the Top 100 as 13-14 year olds remained in the Top 100 as 17-18 year olds.

- Only 17.1% of boys ranked in the Top 100 as 13-14 year olds remained in the Top 100 as 17-18 year olds.

- Only 24.2% of girls ranked in the Top 100 as 15-16 year olds remained in the Top 100 as 17-18 year olds.

- Only 26.5% of boys ranked in the Top 100 as 15-16 year olds remained in the Top 100 as 17-18 year olds.

LATE STARTERS

Swimmers, who get off to a late start in swimming, may believe that success has passed them by, but nothing could be further from the truth. Ed Moses, a world-class breaststroker, did not begin year-round training until his senior year in high school. He went on to win a silver medal at the 2000 Olympic Games. Ed's story is just one of many.

I WANT TO STOP SWIMMING

First off, I do not believe that a child should be permitted to stop swimming or any chosen activity on a whim. If the parent, after careful deliberation, concludes that competitive swimming is a good choice for their child, the child owes the parent an honest and committed effort of one to two years. If, after that period, the child decides that swimming is not for them, they should be allowed to stop to pursue other interests. Committing for this period provides the child with adequate time to benefit from a mental, technical, and physical standpoint. The recommended "try-out period" is also long enough for a child to develop close friendships which are tremendously important in swimming.

EARLY RETIREMENT

All too many swimmers retire from the sport prematurely. Common reasons include:

- Loss of interest
- Unfulfilling
- Lack of fun
- Too much stress
- Boring
- Dysfunctional swimmer-coach relationship
- Lack of time for study, friends, and other activities
- Desire to participate in other sports or non-sport activities
- Lack of inspiration and motivation
- Too time-consuming
- Too much work

RATE OF IMPROVEMENT

Progress or the rate of improvement is the fuel that motivates swimmers to try harder and achieve more; therefore, the ability to measure progress is essential. The most objective and efficient method involves determining the rate of improvement per year based on percentages. Yearly improvement should range between 15-20% for swimmers ages 9-11 and 5-10% for swimmers ages 12-14. For example, if a swimmer had a time of 1:10.0 last year and dropped to 1:03.0 this year their rate of improvement was 10%. If the improvement rate is unacceptable, adjustments must be made. Improvement rates for swimmers 15-years of age and older are typically far less due to a higher level of proficiency.

HIGHS, LOWS, AND PLATEAUS

If one were to track the yearly progress of an elite-level swimmer, he or she would discover periods where performance improved, stayed the same, or declined. Reasons for performance fluctuations vary including a loss of motivation, overtraining, or under-training. Other causes include emotional stress, illness, poor diet, or changes in technique. Whatever the reason, an elite-level swimmer continues to strive knowing that better days are ahead. Case in point, in the two years leading up to the 2012 Olympic Games, Michael Phelps did not post a best time in the 200-butterfly, his signature event.

BALANCING ACT

Swimming can be a real balancing act. In addition to a demanding practice schedule, swimmers must honor family and family obligations while striving for academic excellence. This can be extremely trying at times especially at the height of the swim season. While swimmers may feel obligated or pressured to put swimming first, they must always remember that devotion to family and academic excellence are the two top priorities.

There are four primary factors that contribute to the achievement of best times in competition including emotional well-being, mental skills, technical competence, and physical fitness. Best times can be achieved through improvements in any one of these four factors singularly or in combination.

- Examples of improvements in emotional well-being include increased levels of self-confidence, a belief in a positive outcome, and a greater knowledge of how to effectively deal with the demands that lie ahead.

- Examples of improvements in mental skills include the ability to create a "best time mindset" prior to competing, possessing the focus to follow a racing strategy, and the ability to adapt to unforeseen challenges.

- Examples of improvements in technical competence include a more powerful start, faster turns, and enhanced stroke technique.

- Examples of improvements in physical fitness include increased levels of endurance, strength, and flexibility.

Swimmers who place a high degree of importance on improving one or all of these primary factors significantly increase their chances of achieving best times.

HIGH SCHOOL SWIMMING

Choosing to swim for the high school team can be a difficult choice for club swimmers. On one hand, they want to support their school, but on the other hand, they want to remain loyal to their club team. Conflicts often arise between high school coaches and club coaches in terms of what decisions are best for swimmers over the long term.

The main advantage of remaining with the club revolve around consistency in coaching style, training, teaching, and racing strategies. In addition, swimmers can build a broader aerobic base throughout the season due to less training interruptions allowing for a more extensive taper at the end of the season.

Advantages of high school swimming include heightened team spirit, a change in routine, new learning experiences, and the opportunity to train with different coaches and swimmers. Swimmers may also have a better chance of ranking at the high school level due to a less competitive field.

Ideally, coaches from both sides need to find common ground and cooperate with each other so that swimmers benefit in the end. In a tug of war between coaches, only the swimmers get hurt. Personally, I have met excellent coaches on either side and believe both have much to offer.

COLLEGE SCHOLARSHIPS

The chance of earning a college scholarship is the dream of thousands of age group and senior-level swimmers. Currently, more than 6,000 swimmers in the USA are on full or partial athletic scholarships. Many parents believe that if they send their child to a swim camp at a particular college, their chances of receiving a scholarship at that college increases. Nothing could be further from the truth. Scholarships are awarded to swimmers whose times are competitive within that team and who can score the most points in dual meets and conference championships. For example, a swimmer who dreams of attending Stanford must have times that are compatible. They must also demonstrate a high academic standing to be accepted and remain eligible. The amount of scholarship money a swimmer receives depends on a number of factors including swimming ability and academic achievement. A school may pay the full fare or require the swimmer to make a contribution. In 2014, there were 460 men's college swimming programs in the USA and 580 women's college swimming programs.

To help streamline the process, parents and swimmers must do their homework. They should first look for schools that offer the course of study desired and are located in areas of the country that interest them. Next, they should visit the school's swimming website to see if the swimming times are compatible. If they find a match, they should add it to a preferred list. If not, they should continue researching until finding the right match. Swimmers may contact college coaches at any time although college coaches may not contact swimmers until after July 1 of their junior year of high school. The best way to initiate contact with a college coach is through email as most have their emails listed on the school's website.

SWITCHING TEAMS

Parents often ask my advice on switching teams. I suggest they stay with the current team provided their child is making a reasonable rate of progress year-to-year and enjoys the overall experience. As mentioned previously, yearly rates of improvement differ, but in general, 10-20% for swimmers 9-11 years of age and 5-10% for swimmers 12-14 years of age. Rates of improvement for swimmers 15-years of age and older are typically less. The downside with switching teams is that parents and swimmers may have few options due to a limited amount of swim teams in the area. Another potential disadvantage is a complete reversal in the training approach as they differ from coach to coach. Parents can also earn a reputation for "team jumping" where coaches are reluctant to accept their child.

BIGGER IS NOT ALWAYS BETTER

Joining a big swim team can seem very appealing with a star-studded roster, renowned coaching staff, and a winning record. They typically have greater resources and can provide swimmers with more training and competitive options. In addition, a big team environment can instill a feeling of invincibility within its membership. Many swimmers dream of swimming on a big team and rise to the occasion. However, before joining other factors should be considered. A big swim team can be very impersonal, the result of too many swimmers and too few coaches. Frequently, its reputation is built on the backs of a few star swimmers. Many parents mistakenly believe that the success experienced by the stars will trickle down to their child regardless of ability level. Due to the competitive nature of a big team, the majority of swimmers will never have the opportunity to train with the head coach. In addition, due to overcrowded conditions, practices tend to be more non-stop in nature with higher amounts of yardage and less personalized attention.

SPORT SPECIALIZATION

Most coaches have an opinion as to when children should concentrate solely on swimming versus playing other sports. With that in mind, I conducted my research and turned up some interesting material. The American Academy of Pediatrics recommends that prior to puberty children should participate in multiple sports, but not to the point of overdoing. Early participation in multiple sports leads to better overall motor and athletic development, an increased ability to transfer sports skills to other sports, and enhanced confidence. A study by Ohio State University found that children who specialize early in just one sport were the first to quit. A 2013 American Medical Society for Sports Medicine study found that 88% of college athletes participated in more than one sport as a child. Moreover, a study of 1200 youth athletes by Dr. Neeru Jayanthi of Loyola University found that early specialization in a single sport was one of the strongest predictors of injury. In addition, children who specialize too soon are at greater risk of burnout due to increased stress and a lack of motivation. I advise parents to let their child participate in other sports that compliment swimming until puberty and perhaps beyond. Compatible sports or activities include soccer, gymnastics, dance, cross country running, volleyball, basketball, and the martial arts.

EVENT SPECIALIZATION

A swimmer's "best stroke" can change many times over their career. That is why every age group swimmer should focus on individual medley training, the training of all four strokes, and the racing of all events offered in their age group. Swimmers who are exposed to these three factors early on are in a much better position to compete successfully in whatever stroke(s) or event(s) become their best later on. Research indicates that elite-level swimmers specialize later in their careers and that early specialization can lead to overuse issues, limitations of essential fitness factors, and early burnout.

SWIM CAMPS

Parents often ask my advice on the effectiveness of swim camps and whether they are a wise option for swimmers. In my view, not all swim camps are created equal or provide the catalyst for effective change. A swim camp should focus on swimming needs not addressed by the home team. Most swim teams do an excellent job training swimmers from a physical perspective, but due to overcrowded conditions and understaffing, they lack the ability to provide sufficient technical and mental conditioning. That is where Peak Performance Swim Camp comes into play. We offer a holistic training approach combining mental, technical, and physical conditioning and act as a support system for the home team. The concepts and techniques taught are well-accepted within the swimming community. Our overall objective is to make each swimmer better, and in turn, make each swim team better.

PRIVATE COACHING

If a parent suspects that their child is falling behind in school, they will seek the teacher's assistance. If the teacher is unable to help, the parent may hire a tutor. I believe the same scenario fits in the swimming world. A parent should seek assistance from the coach if they suspect that their child is falling behind particularly in the case of stroke technique. Hopefully, the coach will find a way to help, but if not, parents should seek an outside coach for assistance. Many parents are reluctant to take this step due to fear of reprisal. However, doing nothing is not a solution and only puts swimmers at a greater disadvantage. I have conducted thousands of private lessons and they have produced enormous benefits. When looking for a private coach, parents should ensure that the coach is highly skilled, discreet, and conducts himself or herself in a professional manner.

CHAPTER 2.

EXPAND YOUR KNOWLEDGE

In *The Swimming Triangle*, I introduced the concept of holistic training where swimmers achieve peak performance through a three-sided approach of mental, technical, and physical conditioning. In this book, I want to share the importance of another three-sided approach involving swimmers, coaches, and parents. Parents can play a pivotal role in the swimming success of their child and numerous studies support their involvement. To be of most benefit, parents must stay informed on topics that relate to their child and swimming. A sample of relevant topics appear here.

A LIFE-CHANGING EXPERIENCE

When I look back at my childhood years, I recall two teachers who made a huge difference in my life. They took a deep interest in me, treated me with kindness, and exercised patience. I returned the favor by excelling in their class and becoming a star pupil. Parents should seek out a swim coach who has the potential to impact their child, in the same way.

WORDS OF WISDOM

The following quote is attributed to Jimmy Johnson, the former Head Coach of the Dallas Cowboys. It epitomizes what I believe to be the first rule of coaching:

"Treat a person as he is, and he will remain as he is. Treat a person as if he were where he could be and should be, and he will become what he should be and could be."

A COACH DEFINED

If ten swim coaches were asked to define the word "coach", they would give ten different answers. While each coach is purely one a kind, they fall into three broad categories, including trainer, trainer/teacher, and trainer/teacher/motivator. A trainer focuses exclusively on conditioning the body. A trainer/teacher focuses on conditioning the body and developing the necessary skills. A trainer/teacher/motivator focuses on conditioning the body, developing the necessary skills, and motivating the mind. A swim coach by my definition is a trainer/teacher/motivator. They embrace a holistic approach that engages swimmers from a physical, technical, and mental perspective.

ONE STEP AT A TIME

Self-improvement is best achieved one step at a time. John Wooden, one of the most successful coaches in the history of college basketball once said, "When you improve a little each day, eventually big things occur. Do not look for the big improvement. Seek the small improvement one day at a time. That is the way it happens, and when it happens, it lasts." Parents would be wise to discuss this important concept with their child.

Swim parents are often required to provide guidance and support in a sport they may be unfamiliar. To be most effective, they should educate themselves on the nuances of swimming. To assist, I compiled a list of top recommendations:

- Parents should provide unconditional support to their child. In other words, "We love you whether you win or lose."

- Parents should not belittle their child's fears or concerns. They may seem trivial , but not to the child.

- Parents should give their child the freedom to fail without penalty. Otherwise, the child could become risk averse.

- Parents should be cautious when comparing their child to other swimmers on the team. It may work in the short-term, but it can also backfire.

- Parents should not overextend their child in other activities as swimming is a very demanding and time-consuming sport.

- Parents should find creative and positive ways to motivate their child. Being too strict can take the fun out of swimming and lead to early retirement.

- Parents should encourage their child to build friendships on the team as they are a significant reason children stay in swimming.

- Parents should allow their child the independence needed to find their place on the team.

- Parents should avoid imposing their "swimming wants and wishes" on their child. Ultimately, the level of success attained is determined by the child.

- Parents should find alternative ways to define success in swimming. A constant emphasis on winning or achieving best times can grow old and lead to discouragement.

- Parents should do their research before deciding on a swim team for their child. Choosing the biggest team or a team in proximity to home may not always be the best option.

- Parents should teach the child respect for the coach and to value the coach's opinion.

- Parents should do their utmost to establish a harmonious relationship with their child's coach.

- Parents should give the coach the same support that they give their child.

- Parents should encourage, but not coach their child. Coaching creates conflict, sends mixed messages to the child, and undermines the swimmer-coach relationship.

- Parents should teach their child how "everyday things" can make the big difference. Like attending practice regularly, listening to the coach, and getting to bed on time.

- Parents should immerse themselves in the swimming

culture. I am not suggesting they go overboard, but for the sake of their child they must have a basic understanding of how the swimming world works.

- Parents should stay up to date with swim team happenings.

- Parents should allow their child to travel with the team to out of town competitions where appropriate.

- Parents should assist their child in managing their daily schedule. Striking a healthy balance between school, swimming, and other commitments allows the child to be more productive in swim practice.

- Parents should give their child a complete break from swimming when the schedule permits.

- Parents should do volunteer work for the team.

- Parents should reduce or eliminate junk food from their child's diet and provide fresh, tasty, and healthy food alternatives.

HARMFUL PARENT BEHAVIORS

Having coached most of my life, I am very familiar with harmful parent behaviors that disadvantage the child and puts their swimming at risk. These unwanted behaviors can also harm the coach and team. For the sake of all concerned, I urge parents to avoid them at all cost. Common examples include:

- Causing the child to miss practice.

- Causing the child to miss swim meets.

- Leaving a swim meet before the relays.

- Arriving to practice late.

- Arriving to swim meets late.

- Pulling the child out of practice early.

- Pulling the child out of swim meets early.

- Placing undue pressure on the child.

- Expecting the child to achieve best times at every swim meet.

- Scheduling vacations during championship season.

- Prohibiting the child from participating in team building activities.

- Involving the child in too many outside activities.

- Smothering the child.

- Expecting preferential treatment from the coach.

- Disregarding team rules.

- Coaching the child from the sidelines.

- Thinking they know more about swimming than the coach.

- Avoiding team obligations.

- Questioning every decision the coach makes.

- Complaining constantly.

- Taking the child's side no matter what.

- Blaming the coach and never the child.

- Failing to give the coach or team credit.

CRAZY SWIM PARENTS

For the record, I have met hundreds of great swimming parents over the years. Unfortunately, I have also met my fair share of "crazy swim parents" who possess many of the harmful parental behaviors previously cited, but take it to an extreme level. They fool themselves into believing that it is all about their child, but in reality it is all about them. They push their child to the breaking point and will do anything, even unethical things, to gain the upper hand. On a very rare occasion, I have seen these unfortunate children succeed in swimming, but at a physiological cost. In the end, I wonder whether or not the journey was worth the cost. Crazy swim parent behaviors include:

- Entering their child into swim meets every weekend.

- Emphasizing the need to win, above all else.

- Blaming their child's poor performance on the coach, program, or pool conditions.

- Finding something to criticize in every race.

- Using threats to boost their child's performance.

- Grounding their child after a poor swim meet performance.

- Giving their child the "silent treatment" after a poor swim meet performance.

- Expressing dissatisfaction with their child, no matter how well they do.

- Lecturing their child endlessly.

- Demanding that their 10-year-old train with the senior group.

- Believing their child is a superstar and deserving of preferential treatment.

- Forcing their child to train or compete even when visibly sick.

- Personally training their child on the weekends.

- Forcing the child to train during an official team break.

- Highly critical of the coach, the team, and swimmers on the team.

- Denigrating the coach in public.

- Pitting one coach against another.

- Spreading false and malicious rumors.

- Recruiting other parents to become crazy parents.

INVISIBLE AND VISIBLE

Ideal swim parents are both invisible and visible. By invisible, they stay in the background provided their child is treated with respect, enjoys healthy progress, remains highly motivated, and injury free. By visible, they contact the coach should any of these critical factors change for the worse. While the ideal coach does their utmost to ensure that all swimmers remain happy, healthy, and productive, they may miss a telltale sign of trouble ahead. That is when invisible parents become visible making the coach aware of the situation.

Above all, parents should be courteous when speaking to the coach. Even if the coach fails to respond in kind, showing courtesy and respect establishes the higher ground and sets the right example. If a situation arises, that requires dialog with the coach, parents should not assume they have all the answers or know the whole story. They should give the coach the benefit of the doubt until all of the facts are known. If the coach questions the child's behavior, parents should avoid taking the position that their child is never wrong. Children are human and, therefore, capable of error. While parents are not required to be best friends with the coach, they should establish a rapport and an open line of communication.

PROBLEM SOLVING

The best way to deal with any problem is to tackle it head-on. Through the course of a child's swimming career problems arise. Parents should schedule a meeting with the coach as staying silent typically makes matters worse. A good coach wants happy, healthy, productive, and successful swimmers and will strive to find a favorable solution.

ROLE REVERSAL

In parenting, the parents set the course, and the child follows. As the child matures, parents should willingly hand over the reigns of responsibility provided the child complies. I believe the same process should occur in swimming, especially with younger children. In the beginning, parents should lead ensuring that the child attends all practices, is prepared for training, and participates in all scheduled competitions. As the child matures, parents should willingly hand over greater responsibility provided the child complies.

MY CHILD DOES NOT LISTEN TO ME

Parents are often frustrated by the fact that their child readily dismisses their advice, but accepts the coach's advice as gospel. This reaction may be due to the symbiotic relationship the develops between the child and coach. Other possibilities include gains in knowledge and wisdom on the child's part or the need for independence from the parents.

As the swimmer gains knowledge, experience, and wisdom, the coach frequently finds himself or herself in the same position as parents. To continue advancing the swimmer, they must find alternative ways to advise and guide. One example involves presenting various options to the swimmer and allowing them to make the final decision. In doing so, the coach remains part of the process, but allows the swimmer to feel that their acquired knowledge, experience, and wisdom have value. Parents would be wise to incorporate the same strategy in matters that relate to swimming off the pool deck. Doing so keeps them relevant and in the loop.

PLAY FIRST, WORK SECOND

No doubt swimming is a challenging sport. While the overall experience is awesome, it has its drawbacks in terms of miles of yardage, early morning practices, and marathon swim meets. With that I mind, I believe coaches and parents should encourage younger children to view swimming as play first rather than work. An approach with a focus on play keeps things light, fun, and not so serious. An approach with a focus on work can be joyless, lead to higher levels of stress, and a dislike for the sport. I am not suggesting that coaches encourage younger swimmers to goof off in practice, but rather they should inject some playfulness into the swimming environment.

OVER-COMMITTED

In today's fast-paced world, children are often over-committed. In addition to swimming, they belong to various school groups, church groups, civic groups, participate in other sports, take music lessons, have a tutor, and more. Parents naturally want the best for their child. Unfortunately, what is best for them in a well-rounded sense, is not necessarily the best for them in a swimming sense. Overcommitted swimmers seem exhausted most of the time and in many cases lack focus due to a mind filled with obligations and deadlines. They typically miss more practices than other swimmers and often arrive to practice late or leave early which negatively impacts training. They also go to fewer swim meets and miss out on the thrill, joy, and rewards of competing. While I believe that children should experience other opportunities for their betterment, I also think parents need to walk a fine line if they feel that their child has a future in swimming. What troubles me the most is that overcommitted swimmers never realize their full swimming potential.

EASIER SAID THAN DONE

No doubt, parents want the best for their child, but I am often dismayed by their unrealistic expectations. It is not uncommon for parents to expect their child to drop significant amounts of time at every swim meet or make a "cut" well beyond the child's current reach. Do NFL quarterbacks throw game-winning touchdowns every game or do professional tennis players "ace" every serve? To perform at peak levels, a number of critical factors must merge at a given point in time. Unfortunately, swimmers cannot always control when that occurs. Parents should be pleased with a reasonable rate of progress throughout the year and not go overboard.

A WINNING FORMULA

No two swimmers win a race in the same manner. One may win due to superior size and mental toughness. Another may win due to a superior work ethic and sheer determination. Understanding one's winning attributes can turn self-doubt into self-belief. Parents would be wise to discuss this swimming reality with their child and encourage them to focus on their strengths.

TENACITY

Talent alone cannot guarantee success in the pool. The need to be tenacious or unwilling to let go of a dream, no matter how difficult, is essential particularly in a sport with so many highs and lows. I have observed super-talented swimmers struggle due to a lack of tenacity, and swimmers with less talent thrive because of it. To develop this all-important virtue, parents should discuss the meaning of tenacity with their child and encourage them to persist in all matters.

OLYMPIC DREAM

Virtually every young age group swimmer dreams of going to the Olympics one day. Unfortunately, as years pass many of them downsize their dream. The reason for the change in course varies from swimmer to swimmer. Some of the most common reasons include an unwillingness to commit to the journey, a realization that the dream is beyond one's capabilities, or that the dream is no longer relevant. Whatever the reason, parents should support their child in whatever dream matters to them.

MAGIC PILL

If only I had the genius to create a magic pill that produced amazing results with little effort on the swimmer's part, I would be the greatest coach on the planet! Unfortunately, no magic pill exists, at least to my knowledge, but there is hope. Swimmers can still produce amazing results through the power of self-belief, positivity, and determination.

PRACTICE NUTRITION

There are dozens of sports drinks, gels, bars, and powders on the market each claiming to have discovered the secret to peak performance. If a parent is willing to invest in these high priced items, I recommend the following: a high-carb bar before practice, a sports drink during practice, and a high-protein bar immediately following practice. The high-carb bar provides quick energy for training and the sports drink replaces fluids and electrolytes lost through sweat. The high protein bar aids muscle repair and growth. Additional information on sports nutrition is available in Chapter 5.

CHAPTER 3.

MENTAL MATTERS

THE PROCESS

Olympic swimmers are the net result of a process spanning many years. Most likely, they began as young age groupers with no idea how to read the clock, train in circles, or swim the butterfly. From there, their mental, technical, and physical fitness grew exponentially as they performed multi-mile practices and competed in swim meet after swim meet. From there, they rose to the highest levels of competitive swimming.

Swimmers respond to the process differently. Some thrive on it while other seem overwhelmed by it. As a coach, I have come to realize that the best approach is to be patient and to provide swimmers with the time they need to figure out their place within the process. Many coaches and parents mistakenly believe that swimmers who respond earliest to the process are the ones destined for greatness. On the contrary, I know of many who struggled for years and then went on to swimming stardom.

I advise parents to provide ongoing and unlimited emotional support while nurturing their child's self-belief and confidence. They should assume the role of personal cheerleader and never doubt in their child's ability. I also recommend that they keep things in perspective by putting themselves in their child's shoes. All too often, parents ruin a good thing due to a lack of patience and empathy.

THE TRUTH AND NOTHING BUT

Olympic gold medal gymnast Shannon Miller believes that mental training is the difference-maker in sport. She states that "the physical aspect of the sport can only take you so far. The mental aspect has to kick in, especially if your talking about the best of the best."

IT STARTS HERE

Mahatma Gandhi, the prominent Indian political and spiritual leader, once said, " A man is but a product of his thoughts; what he thinks, he becomes." As parents, you recognize the truth in his words, but a child has little understanding of how thought impacts daily life. Thoughts act like an internal guidance system directing a person toward or away from a desired goal. Positive, determined, and confident thoughts lead to victory while contrary thoughts lead to defeat.

Unfortunately, most coaches stress the importance of the physical far more than the mental. As parents, you must set the record straight and teach your child that all great accomplishments begin with thought that lead to action.

A CASE FOR CONFIDENCE

Confidence is an essential component to success. It is an internal voice that urges us to try and tells us we can. We are born with a full helping of confidence, but it diminishes over time due to the trials and tribulations of life. Each mistake we make lessens it. The same thing occurs when we are criticized, neglected, chastised, teased, or made to feel ashamed. A child who lacks confidence can never achieve the success they deserve in swimming or life. I have encountered many swimmers who possessed the physical and technical attributes to become swimming rock stars, but were thwarted due to a lack of confidence. To reap the benefits that confidence delivers, swimmers must make confidence-building a top priority. Perhaps the famous poem, "The Man Who Thinks He Can" by Walter D. Wintle will underscore my point:

> If you think you are beaten, you are;
> If you think you dare not, you don't.
> If you'd like to win, but think you can't,
> It's almost a cinch you won't.
>
> If you think you'll lose, you're lost,
> For out in the world we find
> Success begins with a fellow's will;
> It's all in the state of mind.
>
> If you think you're outclassed, you are;
> You've got to think high to rise.
> You've got to be sure of yourself before
> You can ever win a prize.
>
> Life's battles don't always go
> To the stronger or faster man;
> But soon or late the man who wins
> Is the man who thinks he can.

* Walter D. Wintle was a poet who lived in the late 19th and early 20th century. Unfortunately, nothing is known of the details of his life. He is best known for writing "The Man Who Thinks He Can".

FAILING IS NOT AN OPTION

In my early forties, I found myself at a crossroads in life where I had to choose between two career paths. One involved returning to the ranks of club coaching that had defined me for more than two decades. The other involved remaining in camp coaching that I truly loved, but presented many challenges. In the end, I chose to stay with what I loved most. Getting the camp off to a successful start proved extremely difficult, but failing was never an option for me. My dogged determination and intense desire to succeed proved to be a winning strategy that allowed me to create Peak Performance Swim Camp. To succeed, swimmers must embrace the same winning strategy, no matter how difficult the path.

GOAL SETTING 101

Much has been written about the importance of goal setting in swimming; its value unquestioned. Goals are like a map, pointing swimmers in the right direction. Goals are like a ruler, measuring their progress along the way. Goals are like a magnet, drawing them ever closer. Goals are a personal matter and must be set by the individual swimmer. While most coaches spend time on goal setting, not all do. Swimmers with firmly established goals achieve far more than those who do not. Parents would be wise to address the topic of goal setting with their child. Without goals, a child is like a ship adrift at sea.

THE BENEFIT OF HARDSHIP

The dictionary defines hardship as a cause of suffering or conditions that make life difficult to bear. History shows that successful people in all walks of life have had to endure their share of hardship on their rise to the top. As difficult as it may be to accept, hardship does have its benefits including gains in wisdom and the development of essential character traits like patience, determination, and mental toughness. The life stories presented here help to illustrate the point:

- Soichiro Honda developed a unique piston ring that he intended to sell to Toyota, but they rejected his invention.

He dealt with his hardships by forming the Honda Motor Corporation.

- Bill Birdseye was the inventor of frozen foods. He discovered the secrets of flash freezing and revolutionized the food processing industry. In pursuit of his vision, he went bankrupt seven times.

- Albert Einstein did not start speaking until the age of four and did not start reading until the age of seven. His teachers and schoolmates saw him as mentally handicapped. Although Einstein got off to a slow start, he became one of the greatest minds in history winning the Nobel Prize for physics.

- Colonel Saunders had his recipe for fried chicken rejected by over a thousand restaurants before opening a chain of restaurants now known as KFC.

- Michael Jordan was cut from his high school basketball team then went on to become one of the greatest basketball players in history.

- George Lucas spent four years sending his Star Wars script to various Hollywood studios and racking up numerous rejection letters. Had he given up, he would not have had the highest grossing film of all time.

- Michael Phelps did not post a best time in the 200-butterfly, his signature event, in the two years leading up to the 2012 Olympics. He went on to win the gold medal in that event and break the world record.

DONKEY IN THE WELL

The following parable sheds additional light on hardship. The author is unknown.

One day a donkey fell into a well. The animal cried and cried as the farmer tried to figure out what to do. He decided that the animal was too old and not worth saving so he asked his neighbors to help him fill in the well. They all grabbed shovels and began shoveling dirt into the well. The donkey realized what was happening and cried horribly. Then, to everyone's amazement he went silent. A few shovel loads later, the farmer looked down into the well to see what was happening and was astonished at what he saw. With each shovel load of dirt that hit the donkey's back, the donkey shook it off and took a step up. As the neighbors continued to shovel dirt into the well, the donkey continued to shake it off and step upward. Finally, to the amazement of all, the donkey reached the top of the well and merrily trotted off.

The moral of the story is that the shovel loads of dirt represented hardships for the donkey. Rather than give up, he used them to rise to the top.

COMMITTED VERSUS INVOLVED

Being committed to a cause is the only sure way to ensure success. Many swimmers mistake involvement for commitment. Involvement means to participate in something while commitment means to be dedicated to something. Committed swimmers are steadfast, resolute, and unstoppable. They are willing to endure any difficulty for the sake of their goal. Involved swimmers lack the resolve that commitment brings and abandon their goal in the face of difficulty. Swimmers will often blame their lack of success on an absence of talent or ability, but in most cases it is due to an absence of commitment.

HUNGER MATTERS

Some swimmers hunger for success while others show little interest. This apparent lack of interest can be very frustrating for dedicated parents. Personally, I showed little interest in swimming when I first started, but as I began to realize my potential my hunger for success grew steadily, and I went on to qualify for the Olympic Trails. Parents should exercise caution before casting judgement on their child. A child's lack of interest may be entirely due to an inability to judge their abilities and potential.

SELF-DISCIPLINE

Success in any endeavor requires a tremendous amount of self-discipline. People who possess self-discipline do not succumb to urges, emotions, bad habits, or outside influences. Instead, they make deliberate choices that reflect and support their short and long-term goals. Swimmers who possess this all-important character trait focus their minds and take action regardless of obstacles, discomfort, or difficulties. Self-discipline also allows swimmers to reach their objectives in a shorter period of time.

FOCUS MATTERS

While seldom touted as a key advantage, the ability to focus or pay attention plays a critical role in peak performance. Swimmers who maintain a high degree of attention throughout practice benefit to a far greater extent. Research indicates that teenage boys are unable to sustain attention for more than twenty-five minutes before a need to refocus. The attention span is even less for younger swimmers.

Attention can be prolonged provided swimmers are highly motivated, have an interest in the task, and feel capable. Fatigue, hunger, emotional stress, and a distracting learning environment can also have detrimental effects on focus.

Focus also plays a significant role in competition. Swimmer Mark Gangloff, a two-time Olympian and Olympic Gold Medalist states: "As you move further and further down the line, the mental game becomes even more important than physical preparation. At the top, everyone has the same physical attributes, but it's whether or not you are mentally prepared to race that matter most." Gangloff identified the ability to focus as the premier mental skill of top level swimmers. "To me. it's the ability to focus your energies and stay within your race plan."

VISUALIZE TO MAXIMIZE

The science of visualization is one of the most effective methods to boost swimming performance yet few swimmers take advantage of it. The process involves using the imagination to achieve a desired outcome. The science behind it is fascinating. When the brain consistently sees something it desires, neural connections form within the brain and the likelihood of obtaining the desired outcome increases significantly. Swimmers who visualize themselves executing a near-perfect race plan are far more likely to achieve it. The expression, "If you can see it, you can be it" fits beautifully with the science of visualization. The following quote underscores the value of visualization:

"I've been visualizing myself every night for the past four years, standing on the podium, having the gold medal placed around my neck." — Megan Quann – 2000 Olympic Gold Medal Swimmer

EXCITE TO IGNITE

When excited, swimmers become ignited. Excitement and the ignition that follows supplies the motivational fuel to survive and thrive in the demanding world of competitive swimming. Excitement comes from various sources including stimulating practices, positive results, inspirational coaches, and supportive parents. All too often I encounter swimmers who lack excitement and, as a consequence, underperform. I believe that swimmers perform far better when their fitness levels and excitement levels match. Parents should monitor their child to ensure excitement levels remain high throughout the year. Periodic dips in excitement are a natural part of the swimming process. A lack of excitement over an extended period could be an early warning sign of potential burn out.

THREE KINDS OF SWIMMERS

While no two swimmers are alike, they fall into three broad categories including "workhorse swimmers", "racehorse swimmers", and "workhorse/racehorse swimmers". Workhorse swimmers work extremely hard in practice, but generally fail to swim up to expectations in competition. Racehorse swimmers soar in competition, but generally fail to work up to their potential in practice. Workhorse/racehorse swimmers represent the best of both, working hard in practice and excelling in competition. Elite-level swimmers belong to the latter group. To improve the performance levels of workhorse swimmers, the coach should assist in developing a pre-race mental game plan to reduce anxiety levels and improve focus ability. Parents must also refrain from adding additional pressure. To improve the performance levels of racehorse swimmers, the coach must increase their appetite for hard work.

TRAIN SMART, RACE STUPID

Elite-level swimmers compete with few thoughts in their heads. They race on auto-pilot, their starts, strokes, turns, finishes, and racing strategies automated through thoughtful and repetitive practice. By the time the race rolls around thinking narrows to just a few thoughts.

OVER THINK, UNDER PERFORM

Swimming is a thinking sport with the need to excel a constant theme. While a thoughtful approach is essential, too much thought can lead to "paralysis through over-analysis". It is not uncommon to find swimmers frozen in thought on the block and unable to access their full mental, technical, and physical capabilities. Overthinking is epidemic in swimming and a significant performance inhibitor. All desired beliefs, skills, and strategies must be automated within the practice setting and prior to the competition. Once swimmers arrive at the block, their minds should be free and clear.

TMI

The acronym "TMI" stands for Too Much Information. Well-meaning parents are often guilty of supplying their child with too much information prior to the competition. I often ask PEAK campers to raise their hands if they forget everything they were told by their parents once the race gets underway. Not surprisingly, every hand is raised. As stated in the previous piece, "all desired beliefs, skills, and strategies must be automated within the practice setting and prior to the competition". Adding last minute instructions may benefit the parents, but it does nothing to help the child.

ADVERSITY

Adversity crosses the path of all swimmers and their ability to handle it determines how quickly they rebound from it. When the Seattle Seahawks lost in the Super Bowl in the final minute of play, their star quarterback, Russell Wilson, stated that he would use the loss to help him to win again. Through tough times, one grows wiser and more successful in the future. Swimmers should view their adversities as opportunities for growth and self-improvement.

BREATHE

Deliberate breathing can help relax swimmers prior to competing. The technique involves breathing slowly, deeply, and with purpose. As a guide, swimmers should perform five breaths per minute; four seconds to inhale, four seconds to exhale, and four seconds to experience the benefit. It is an easy way to relax and create the ideal mental state.

OVERCOMING WORRY

Teaching the mental skills needed to succeed in swimming can be a daunting task. If one were to identify the most important skill, overcoming worry in competition would be at the top of the list. At a recent PEAK clinic, I asked swimmers to raise their hand if they felt that worry interfered with their performance, and all but one swimmer raised their hand. With a response like that, it is easy to understand why worry is a crafty opponent that must be overcome. Swimmers who allow worry to get the better of them are subject to one poor performance after the next. It does not matter how physically fit they are, once worry takes over the body tightens up like a knot.

Well-meaning parents and coaches often tell swimmers not to worry. Typically, this tactic backfires as worry-levels increase even more. In my experience, one of the most effective ways to deal with worry is through the use of distraction. Whenever I go to a movie, my worries are suspended. The same thing occurs when I walk my dogs, listen to music, or dine out with good friends. Distraction is one of the greatest cures for a worried mind.

Swimmers, who are overcome by worry, should have a diversion plan in place that either eliminates or reduces the amount of worry experienced in competition. Examples include texting family and friends, reading, striking up a conversation with teammates, playing video games, meditating, or stretching. It does not matter what swimmers choose provided it fulfills the objective.

NEAR PERFECTION

Perfectionism is the belief that anything less than perfect is unacceptable. While a noble goal, it is fraught with danger and against all odds. Swimmers who strive for perfection or parents who seek perfection from their child may find that it does more harm than good, leading to feelings of anxiety and a lack of fulfillment. Vince Lombardi, one of the most successful American football coaches of all time, once said, "Perfection is not attainable, but if we chase perfection we can catch excellence."

DUMP A SLUMP

A slump is the inability to achieve best times in competition. Virtually all swimmers experience one or more slumps in their career. As previously mentioned, Michael Phelps, the greatest swimmer of all-time, experienced a significant downturn in performance prior to the 2012 Olympic Games.

The contributing causes of a slump are numerous and include undue fatigue, stress, mental barriers, a spate of poor performances, over-training, under-training, illness, injury, and life-changing events. Swimmers typically respond to a slump by becoming discouraged and giving up or by becoming more determined and trying harder. As one might expect, giving up is never the solution. Trying harder is the best response and a significant first step. However, it is not enough on its own. I recently came upon a Zen story that illustrates my point:

A martial arts student went to his teacher and said earnestly, "I am devoted to studying your martial arts system. How long will it take me to master it?" The teacher's reply was casual, "Ten years." Impatiently, the student answered, "But I want to master it faster than that. I will work very hard. I will practice every day, ten or more hours a day if I must. How long will it take then?" The teacher thought for a moment and replied, "20 years."

As illustrated by the teacher's comments, patience plays a major role in overcoming any challenge. Swimmers who are experiencing a slump must exercise patience while addressing all of the contributing causes. For example, if fatigue is the cause, they must get more rest or if stress is the cause, they must find ways to destress. For this reason, the need for patience is absolute.

CHAPTER 4.

TECHNIQUE MATTERS

TECHNIQUE BEFORE TRAINING

Imagine the impact on children who never learned how to read or write, the negative repercussions would haunt them for a lifetime. The same holds true for swimmers who never had the opportunity to learn the proper start, stroke, and turn technique; the adverse effects would haunt them for a swimming lifetime.

A practice common amongst swim teams is to provide swimmers with a window of opportunity to learn proper start, stroke, and turn technique before transitioning to more intense training. The technical window can vary in length depending on the coach's overall philosophy. I know of some coaches who transition their swimmers by the age of 11 or 12 while others by 13 or 14. Regardless of the time frame given, the window of opportunity to learn proper technique eventually closes whether swimmers are technically ready or not. Moreover, those who are not ready suffer the consequences.

In my experience, the vast majority of swimmers lack essential technical skills and compensate by working physically harder. While hard work can mask a lack of technical expertise, over the short term, in the end swimmers suffer and fail to maximize their potential. What can parents do to address this pervasive problem? I recommend sending their child to a top rated swim camp like Peak Performance that specializes in technique. Other options include arranging private lessons with a qualified coach or moving to a team that places a greater emphasis on technique. On a side note, it is not uncommon for coaches to tell parents that technical errors naturally fix themselves overtime. I contend that this view is absolute nonsense. Swimmers must be taught the proper techniques and then given the opportunity to form correct habits in practice.

385 AND COUNTING

The amount of technical know-how in swimming is mind-boggling. By the time swimmers arrive at the elite level, they have perfected three starts, four strokes, seven turns, and four finishes. Each start includes at least four parts with a minimum of five technical points per part. Each stroke consists of at least five parts with a minimum of ten technical points per part. Each turn consists of at least three parts with a minimum of five technical points per part. Each finish consists of at least one part with a minimum of five technical points per part. Added together it represents a total of 385 technical points! The learning of each point is critical to peak performance.

TECHNIQUE, TECHNIQUE, TECHNIQUE

Swim parents invest much time, effort, money, and emotion into their child's swimming. In fairness, I believe parents have a right to know if their child is being taught correctly as proper technique is a key to long-term swimming success.

Many swim parents are surprised to learn that Olympic swimmers enjoy a 75% technical advantage over the average competitive swimmer. No doubt, these swimmers began learning essential skills as young age groupers.

Some parents may find the technical side of swimming somewhat dull, but they should view it similarly as the disciplines of adding, subtracting, multiplying and dividing. Students who master these four disciplines move on to higher levels of mathematics while those who do not remain at the rudimentary level. The same thing occurs in swimming. Swimmers who master the various start, stroke, and turn techniques move on to higher levels of competition while those who do not remain at the developmental level.

I strongly urge parents to observe their child in practice and competition to determine whether the correct skills are being taught. I am not suggesting that parents become overly involved or assume the position of coach, however, as parents, they are ultimately responsible for their child's development. As mentioned previously, the vast majority of coaches truly care about their swimmers and do their utmost to ensure that correct skills are being taught. Unfortunately, due to different training philosophies, overcrowding, understaffing, and challenges in learning some swimmers do miss out. That is where parents must intervene. Should they find that their child is not progressing at a reasonable rate, they should arrange a meeting with the coach and respectfully discuss their concerns. Doing nothing is not a viable alternative.

TECHNICAL NUTS AND BOLTS

The following ten part swimming technique section contains background information and highlights. Sections include the front and back start, butterfly, backstroke, breaststroke, and freestyle. The butterfly, backstroke, breaststroke, and freestyle turns are also included. Parents should refer to the technical highlights when observing their child in the pool. The highlights are universal and intended for swimmers of all levels.

FRONT START — INTRODUCTION

The front start is the fastest part of any race. Unfortunately, the majority of age group swimmers have inferior front starts. There are numerous styles of front starts used in competitive swimming. For the sake of expediency, the Throw & Go Start is outlined here. It is easy to learn and contains all of the essential ingredients that make a great start. Ideally, swimmers should be able to perform a proper front start within the first year of joining a swim team, and the coach should provide extra help to those who struggle. An excellent front start is a prerequisite for college swimming.

FRONT START — HIGHLIGHTS

- When assuming the Take Your Mark Position, the hands grip the front edge of the block just outside the feet.

- For age group swimmers, the primary objective of holding the block is for balance and stability.

- Many advanced age group swimmers use the arms to pull themselves forward off the block.

- Pulling off the block is an advanced skill and is not recommended for the initial learning of the Throw & Go Start.

- When assuming the Take Your Mark Position, the arms remain straight or slightly bent.

- Determining the ultimate amount of elbow bend is an individual preference.

- The feet position on the block shoulder width apart.

- When assuming the Take Your Mark Position, the legs split with one foot placed at the front of the block and the other foot positioned approximately one-foot length behind the front foot.

- To avoid slippage, the toes of the front foot wrap around the front edge of the block.

- The strongest leg is set at the rear of the block when assuming the Take Your Mark Position to generate a more powerful drive off the block.

- Some swimmers prefer to place the strongest leg in the front. I have seen great starts performed from either leg position.

- The heel of the back foot is raised upward with the ball of the foot resting on the block.

- Swimmers drive off the block with the ball of the foot, as the ball is the most explosive part.

- When assuming the Take Your Mark Position, the knees

should bend just enough to allow the hands (or fingers) to grab the block.

- Excessive knee bend results in squatting on the block causing a loss of driving power.

- Determining the ultimate amount of knee bend is an individual preference.

- To increase driving power off the block, swimmers should add plyometric training to their dry-land training routine.

- Plyometrics involves a series of explosive jumping movements using only body weight.

- The straight arms throw to head height or beyond as the swimmer departs the block, and the legs drive forcefully off the block.

- Forcibly throwing the arms to head height or beyond sends the body outward off the block rather than downward toward the water.

- Arms that point too far downward carry the body downward resulting in a deep dive.

- The most common error in a front start is diving too deep which sets off a chain reaction of other errors. Swimmers who dive too deep begin the race from behind.

- The arms and legs should achieve a full streamline position in the air prior to entering the water.

- The body should enter the water in a straight diagonal line with no bending at the waist.

- The body should enter the water fingertips first and toe tips last.

- Experience plays a significant role in the quality of a front start.

- The more often swimmers have the opportunity to practice quality front starts in practice, the more likely they will execute them in a competition.

FRONT START INTO BUTTERFLY — HIGHLIGHTS

- The body should enter the water fingertips first and toe tips last. At no time should the body pike.

- Swimmers should enter the water with the entire body in a 100% streamline position.

- Swimmers are permitted to remain completely submerged for a distance of no more than 15-meters off a butterfly start. By that point, the head must break the surface.

- Most age group swimmers travel less than half that distance.

- Swimmers should execute the butterfly underwater travel sequence, upon entering the water, consisting of a streamline phase, a body whip phase, and a breakout phase.

- The head should never lift out of streamline during the entire underwater travel sequence.

- A minimum of three body whips (butterfly kicks) should be performed off a butterfly start, and swimmers who excel at body whip should do more.

- Body whip can be faster than swimming butterfly over a short distance.

- Swimmers should add a butterfly pull to speed up the breakout.

- Pulling to the surface puts swimmers into the flow of butterfly.

- Ideally, the body should be on the surface and fully horizontal at the completion of the butterfly pull.

- Swimmers should transition seamlessly from the underwater portion of the start to the swimming portion.

- No breath should be taken on the first stroke off the start to ensure a smooth transition.

FRONT START INTO BREASTSTROKE — HIGHLIGHTS

- The body should enter the water fingertips first and toe tips last. At no time should the body pike.

- Swimmers should enter the water with the entire body in a 100% streamline position.

- Unlike the butterfly, backstroke, and the freestyle start, there is no restriction as to how far swimmers are allowed to travel off a breaststroke start.

- Most age group swimmers travel between five and ten yards and surface three to five seconds after entering the water.

- Swimmers should execute the breaststroke underwater travel sequence, upon entering the water, consisting of a streamline phase, a pulldown phase, and a kick-up phase.

- The head should never lift out of streamline during the entire underwater travel sequence.

- On the streamline phase, swimmers maintain a 100% streamline position and hold for one-second to take advantage of the momentum gained from the start.

- On the pulldown phase, swimmers pull the arms down to the sides of the body pressing the palms on the thighs.

- Upon reaching the sides of the body, that arms move quickly forward to initiate the kick-up phase.

- Pausing the hands at the sides of the body causes a loss of forward momentum.

- Advanced-age group swimmers draw the shoulders together at the completion of the pulldown to further reduce drag.

- Ideally, swimmers should begin angling upward toward the surface during the pulldown phase.

- The pulling pattern used in the pulldown resembles a narrow butterfly pull as a wide pull increases drag.

- Swimmers may execute a butterfly kick at any point during the pulldown phase.

- A butterfly kick is optional, but can add additional speed.

- On the kick-up phase, swimmers draw the arms forward under the body into a streamline position.

- As the arms slide forward, the heels rise to the butt.

- A breaststroke kick is performed once the heels reach the height of the butt.

- The kick should be narrow to reduce drag.

- Ideally, the top of the head should break the surface upon the completion of the kick-up phase.

- No gap should exist between the end of the kick-up and the first above water stroke.

- Ideally, the body should be on the surface and fully horizontal at the end of the kick-up phase.

- Swimmers should transition seamlessly from the underwater portion of the start to the swimming portion.

FRONT START INTO FREESTYLE — HIGHLIGHTS

- The body should enter the water fingertips first and toe tips last. At no time should the body pike.

- Swimmers should enter the water with the entire body in a 100% streamline position.

- Swimmers are permitted to remain completely submerged for a distance of no more than 15-meters off a freestyle start. By that point, the head must break the surface.

- Most age group swimmers travel less than half that distance.

- Swimmers should execute the freestyle underwater travel sequence, upon entering the water, consisting of a streamline phase, a body whip phase, and a breakout phase.

- The head should never lift out of streamline during the entire underwater travel sequence.

- A minimum of three body whips (butterfly kicks) should be performed with a freestyle start and swimmers who excel at body whip should do more.

- Swimmers are not disqualified should they choose not to perform body whip off a freestyle start.

- Body whip can be faster than freestyle over a short distance.

- Swimmers should add a freestyle pull combined with freestyle kick to speed up the breakout.

- Pulling to the surface puts swimmers into the flow of freestyle.

- Ideally, the body should be on the surface and fully horizontal at the completion of the freestyle pull.

- Swimmers should transition seamlessly from the underwater portion of the start to the swimming portion.

- No breath should be taken on the first stroke off the start to ensure a smooth transition.

BACK START — INTRODUCTION

The back start is the fastest part of a backstroke race. Unfortunately, the majority of age group swimmers have inferior back starts. The two most common backstroke starts include the Conventional Start and the Japanese Start. For ease of understanding, the Conventional Start is outlined below. References to the Japanese Start are included where appropriate. Ideally, swimmers should be able to perform a proper back start within the first year of joining a swim team, and the coach should provide extra help to those who struggle. An excellent back start is a prerequisite for college swimming.

BACK START — HIGHLIGHTS

- The biggest difference between the two starts occurs when swimmers assume the Take Your Mark Position. In the Conventional Start, swimmers assume a fetal or small ball position drawing closely to the wall. In the Japanese Start, swimmers tilt the head back, keep the back flat, and remain further from the wall.

- Typically, swimmers choose the start that they perform best. Some feel they generate more power via the Conventional Start. Others feel they depart the block quicker via the Japanese Start.

- Due to strength limitations and the fear of slipping, some swimmers prefer not to use the starting block and choose a Gutter Start instead.

- The Gutter Start is an excellent alternative for developing age group swimmers, however, to remain competitive they will need to switch to a block start at some point.

- Using the block allows swimmers to travel further through the air before entering the water thus reducing drag.

- When assuming the Take Your Mark Position, the hands grip the bar shoulder width apart, and the arms typically bend 90-degrees or more.

- Determining the ultimate amount of elbow bend is an individual preference.

- Bending the elbows draws the upper body and hips closer to the surface.

- The final resting place for the hips, relative to the surface, is dependent upon the amount of elbow and knee bend.

- Typically, the more elbow bend, the higher the hips and the more knee bend, the lower the hips.

- Determining the ultimate amount of elbow bend and knee bend is an individual preference.

- Raising the hips too high can cause the feet to slip off the wall.

- When assuming the Take Your Mark Position, the legs typically bend 90-degrees or more.

- The feet position on the wall shoulder width apart.

- The feet also place side-by-side or staggered with one foot slightly higher than the other.

- If staggered, the foot of the strongest leg assumes the higher position on the wall.

- When assuming the Take Your Mark Position, the tips of the toes may appear out of the water, but not curl over the lip of the pool.

- The balls of the feet rest on the wall.

- Determining the ultimate choice of foot position is an individual preference.

- When assuming the Take Your Mark Position in a Conventional Start, the upper body curls into a fetal position with the chin tucked slightly toward the chest.

- When assuming the Take Your Mark Position in a Japanese Start, the head remains tilted backward with the back assuming a "flat back position".

- On a Conventional Start, the head snaps back, the hands release from the block, the arms travel to a streamline position behind the head as the hips snap upward, and the toes throw upward.

- On a Japanese Start, the hands release from the block, the arms travel to a streamline position behind the head as the hips snap upward, and the toes throw upward.

- To shorten the distance traveled by the arms, swimmers may bend the elbows as the arms throw back into streamline.

- Keeping the arms straight or bending the elbows as they release from the block is an individual preference.

- The "head back-hip snap-toe throw sequence" raises the hips and feet out of the water setting up the ideal entry position and reducing drag.

- Most age group swimmers lack the strength to raise the upper and lower body out of the water.

- To increase upper and lower body strength, swimmers should add upper body exercises and plyometrics to their dry-land training routine.

- Plyometrics involves a series of explosive jumping movements using only body weight.

- Most age group swimmers lack the flexibility to arch the back properly.

- To increase flexibility, swimmers should add hip and lower back exercises to their dry-land training routine.

- The body enters the water fingertips first and toe tips last.

- Swimmers should enter the water with the entire body in a 100% streamline position.

- Swimmers are permitted to remain completely submerged for a distance of no more than 15-meters off a backstroke start. By that point, the head must break the surface.

- Most age group swimmers travel less than half that distance.

- Swimmers should execute the backstroke underwater travel sequence, upon entering the water, consisting of a streamline phase, a body whip phase, and a breakout phase.

- The head should never lift out of streamline during the entire underwater travel sequence.

- A minimum of three body whips (butterfly kicks) are performed off a backstroke start, and swimmers who excel at body whip should do more.

- Swimmers are not disqualified should they choose not to perform body whip off a backstroke start.

- Body whip can be faster than backstroke over a short distance.

- Swimmers should add a backstroke pull combined with backstroke kick to speed up the breakout.

- Pulling to the surface puts swimmers into the flow of backstroke.

- Ideally, the body should be on the surface and fully horizontal at the completion of the backstroke pull.

- Swimmers should transition seamlessly from the underwater portion of the start to the swimming portion.

BUTTERFLY — INTRODUCTION

Butterfly is the second fastest stroke and is the most fish-like of all the strokes. Unfortunately, the majority of age group swimmers struggle with the butterfly due to poor technique, a lack of strength or flexibility, or a lack of opportunity to train it. Swimmers who require additional strength or flexibility should add upper and lower body strength and flexibility exercises to their daily dry-land training routine. Ideally, swimmers should be able to perform legal butterfly within the first eighteen months of joining a swim team, and the coach should provide extra help to those who struggle. An excellent butterfly is a prerequisite for college swimming.

BUTTERFLY — HIGHLIGHTS

- From the beginning of the first arm pull in the butterfly, swimmers must remain on the chest.

- Both arms must be brought forward simultaneously over the water and pull back simultaneously under the water.

- All up and down movements of the legs and feet must be simultaneous.

- The position of the legs and feet do not have to be on the same level, but they may not alternate as in the freestyle kick.

- A scissors or breaststroke kicking action is not permitted.

- The dolphin-like action in the butterfly comes from the chest press and the kick.

- Ideally, swimmers should press the chest downward toward the bottom of the pool as the arms enter the water to begin the pull.

- The chest should press down sufficiently to raise the hips out of the water.

- The dolphin-like action aids in propulsion and body position.

- The arms are the primary source of propulsion in the butterfly.

- The arms should enter the water directly in front of the shoulders at full length and from here the pull begins.

- Entry of the hands should be fingertips first or with the palms facing slightly outward.

- The pull is divided into the catch and the finish, and both are primary sources of propulsion.

- In the catch, the elbows bend near 90-degrees and point upward toward the surface of the water as the hands and forearms engage the water and pull the body forward.

- The catch should take place before the shoulders.

- In the finish, the arms accelerate past the hips until fully extended and push the body forward.

- Most age group swimmers lack both a proper catch and a finish due to a lack of skill or strength.

- To increase strength, swimmers should add upper body strengthening exercises to their dry-land training routine.

- The fully extended arms exit the water and travel forward

close to the surface before re-entering the water in front of the shoulders.

- The ideal recovery is shoulder-led with the elbows remaining straight.

- There are two kicks per stroke in the butterfly, one when the arms enter the water and one when the arms exit the water.

- Typically, the second kick is bigger than the first.

- Many age group swimmers lack a second kick due to poor technique.

- The breath occurs early in the stroke as the arms transition into the catch phase of the pull and continues until the arms approach the shoulders during the recovery phase.

- To breathe, swimmers gently push the chin forward as the arms move into the catch phase.

- The head never lifts in the butterfly and the chin never leaves the water.

- Many age group swimmers begin the breath much later in the stroke and closer to the hips. Breathing at this point throws off the timing of the stroke.

- Swimmers who breathe late also tend to keep the head up longer for air.

- Ideally, the head should drop below the surface as the arms approach the shoulders.

- Olympic butterfly swimmers appear "headless" at this point in the stroke as their heads are below the surface of the water.

- Breathing every other stroke is the most common breathing

pattern used, but some swimmers prefer breathing every stroke. Both have merit.

- Breathing every other stroke encourages a better flow while breathing every stroke provides more oxygen.

- In the 50 distance, swimmers may choose to breathe when needed.

- The timing in the butterfly is continuous, meaning there is no beginning or end to the stroke.

- Many age group swimmers pause the arms at the entry point wasting valuable momentum. Pausing is an acute stroke error and must be corrected in the early stages.

BACKSTROKE — INTRODUCTION

Backstroke is the third fastest stroke and is the only stroke swum on the back. There are few rules that govern the backstroke other than the fact that swimmers must remain on the back after the start and each turn. Ideally, swimmers should be able to perform a legal backstroke within the first year of joining a swim team, and the coach should provide extra help to those who struggle. An excellent backstroke is a prerequisite for college swimming.

BACKSTROKE — HIGHLIGHTS

- Ideally, swimmers should maintain a horizontal body position from head to toe when swimming the backstroke with the hips near the surface of the water.

- Keeping the head back and perfectly still with the eyes facing skyward assist swimmers in keeping the hips up.

- Tilting the head forward, an everyday practice, causes the hips to sink and the knees to bend more than desired.

- Many age group swimmers are uncomfortable with keeping the head back and still as they are unable to see where they are going.

- Swimming straight without looking is key in the backstroke.

- Rotation is also part of the backstroke body position.

- As the right arm enters the water, the body should rotate slightly to the right and vice verse.

- The ideal amount of rotation causes the shoulder to clear the surface of the water.

- Shoulder flexibility plays a significant role in the backstroke and swimmers should add shoulder flexibility exercises to their dry-land training routine.

- Ideally, the kick should be narrow and continuous with the right and left leg matching.

- At no time should the knees or feet break the surface.

- The arms should enter the water directly in line with the shoulders, at full length, and from here the pull begins.

- The hands enter the water pinkie first.

- The arms are the primary source of propulsion in the backstroke.

- The pull is divided into the catch and the finish, and both are primary sources of propulsion.

- In the catch, the elbows bend 90-degrees as the hands and forearms engage the water and pull the body forward.

- The catch should take place before the shoulders.

- Most age group swimmers lack the proper catch due to poor technique.

- In the finish, the arms accelerate past the hips until fully straight.

- The fully extended arm exits the water traveling upwards and forwards over the shoulder and back to the entry point.

- The timing of the arms is known as opposite arm timing where one arm remains totally opposite the other.

- The arms must remain seamless or without pause throughout each stroke cycle.

Breaststroke is the fourth fastest stroke. Unfortunately, the majority of age swimmers struggle with breaststroke due to poor technique, a lack of strength or flexibility, or a lack of opportunity to train it. Ideally, swimmers should be able to perform a legal breaststroke within the first year of joining a swim team, and the coach should provide extra help to those who struggle. An excellent breaststroke is a prerequisite for college swimming.

- All movements of the arms in the breaststroke shall be simultaneous and in the same horizontal plane.

- During each breaststroke stroke cycle, some part of the swimmer's head must break the surface of the water.

- The feet must be turned outward during the propulsive phase of the breaststroke kick.

- Scissors, alternating movements, or downward butterfly kicks are not permitted within the stroke.

- Breaking the surface of the water with the feet is allowed unless followed by a downward butterfly kick.

- The kick is the primary source of propulsion in the breaststroke.

- External hip rotation and the ability to rotate the feet so that the big toes are facing out to the sides is key to a fast breaststroke.

- Swimmers who lack these two essential flexibility components struggle with the breaststroke.

- To improve, swimmers should add hip and ankle flexibility exercises to their dry-land training routine.

- Breaststroke is often performed with the incorrect timing.

- Pull, breathe, kick, streamline is the correct timing sequence.

- The only pause within the breaststroke stroke cycle takes place at the end of the streamline phase.

- Frequently, swimmers will pause the arms during the breath, but this is incorrect.

- Swimmers should streamline and assume a streamlined and horizontal body position at the end of each stroke with the head fully or partially tucked between the arms.

- Streamlining at the end of each stroke maximizes the momentum generated by the kick and makes the stroke far more efficient.

- Proper streamlining at the end of each stroke also position the arms correctly for the pull.

- The breaststroke pull consists of three parts including an outward sweeping action beyond shoulder width, an inward sculling action toward the chin line, and a forward shooting action into streamline.

- The arms remain straight on the sweep, bend on the scull, and straighten on the shoot.

- When sculling inward, the elbows should point upward rather than backward.

- When shooting forward, the hands follow the waterline.

- The pull remains forward of the shoulders at all times.

- The head rises for the breath during the inward sculling action of the arms.

- The head lowers as the hands shoot forward.

- The legs are the primary source of propulsion in the breaststroke.

- The heels rise to initiate the kick as the upper body rises for the breath.

- As the heels rise to the butt, the big toes point outward and the legs drive backward to execute the kick.

- The breaststroke kick is more narrow than wide with the knee spread no wider than the width of a basketball.

- To generate greater power, swimmers should snap the feet together at the completion of the kick.

- Swimmers return to a streamlined body position upon completing the kick and hold for one-second.

FREESTYLE — INTRODUCTION

Freestyle is the fastest stroke. By definition, freestyle means any style other than butterfly, backstroke, or breaststroke. Ideally, swimmers should be able to perform legal freestyle within the first year of joining a swim team, and the coach should provide extra help to those who struggle. An excellent freestyle is a prerequisite for college swimming.

FREESTYLE — HIGHLIGHTS

- Ideally, swimmers should maintain a horizontal body position from head to toe when swimming the freestyle with the hips near the surface of the water.

- The head may tilt slightly upward; however too much upward tilt causes the hips to sink.

- The head must also remain still unless turning for a breath.

- Rotation is also part of the freestyle body position.

- As the right arm enters the water, the body should rotate slightly to right and vice verse.

- The ideal amount of rotation causes the shoulder to clear the surface of the water.

- Ideally, the kick should be narrow and continuous with the right and left leg matching.

- At no time should the feet break the surface.

- Breaking the surface causes the feet to lose water pressure and propulsion.

- The majority of age group swimmers kick with their feet out of the water, but this is not correct. Kicking with the feet out is similar to drawing the propellor of a motorboat out of the water.

- The arms are the primary source of propulsion in the freestyle.

- The arms should enter the water directly in line with the shoulders at full length and from here the pull begins.

- The hands enter the water fingertips first.

- The pull is divided into the catch and the finish, and both are primary sources of propulsion.

- In the catch, the elbows bend near 90-degrees and point upward toward the surface of the water as the hands and forearms engage the water and pull the body forward.

- The catch should take place before the shoulders.

- In the finish, the arms accelerate past the hips until fully extended and push the body forward.

- Most age group swimmers lack both a proper catch and a finish due to a lack of skill or strength.

- To increase strength, swimmers should add upper body strengthening exercises to their dry-land training routine.

- Once the finish is complete, the arm typically exits the water elbow first (high elbow recovery).

- Swimmers may also choose to exit the arm from the water straight or slightly bent.

- All three methods are performed at the Olympic level.

- The most common is the high elbow recovery and is recommended for most swimmers.

- The recovery of the arms should be symmetrical with the right and left arm matching.

- The arms recover past the shoulder and back to the entry point.

- The most common timing of the arms is known as catch-up timing where one arm slightly overlaps the other.

- Another form of stroke timing is known as opposite arm timing where one arm remains totally opposite the other.

- Swimmers may breathe to one side or both.

- For the purpose of balance and propulsion issues, breathing every three strokes is recommended for training.

- Breathing should be slight and to the side with the lower goggle in contact with the water.

- As the right arm pulls past the right shoulder, the head turns to the right. As the right arm recovers past the right shoulder, the head turns back to center.

- The same sequence of events occurs when breathing to the left side.

- Breathing patterns change depending on the racing distance.

- In the 50 distance, breathing should be as needed.

- In events longer than a 50, breathing should be more frequent to supply swimmers with greater amounts of oxygen.

SHOCKING!

At a recent PEAK clinic, my staff took underwater footage of 33 swimmers performing freestyle. Once the videotaping was complete, I conducted an individual video review with each swimmer. I was shocked to find that no swimmer performed the high elbow catch correctly – an essential component to fast freestyle! The group consisted of young age groupers, seasoned veterans, and two international-level swimmers.

BUTTERFLY TURN — INTRODUCTION

The butterfly turn is the second fastest part of a butterfly race. Unfortunately, the majority of age group swimmers have inferior butterfly turns. A butterfly turn should seem like an extension of the swim. In other words, the swim should flow smoothly into the turn, and the turn should flow smoothly into the swim. Ideally, swimmers should be able to perform a legal butterfly turn within the first year of joining a swim team, and the coach should provide extra help to those who struggle. An excellent butterfly turn is a prerequisite for college swimming.

BUTTERFLY TURN — HIGHLIGHTS

- Swimmers should begin planning the butterfly turn at the flags and not at the wall as waiting until then leaves no time for last minute adjustments.

- When approaching the wall, there should be no gap between the final stroke and the turn.

- The majority of age group swimmers have a gap due to a lack of knowledge and experience on how to plan for the wall.

- The gap between the last stroke and the wall causes swimmers to decelerate into the wall.

- Another common error involves getting too close to the wall on the final stroke which causes a momentary pause on the wall.

- The speed swimmers maintain into the wall determines the overall speed of the turn.

- The average speed of a practice turn is far below that of a competition turn.

- Swimmers who do not perform fast turns in practice are disadvantaged in competition.

- The more often swimmers have the opportunity to practice race pace turns in practice, the greater the confidence and proficiency level in competition.

- Swimmers must touch the wall entirely on the chest.

- Both hands must touch the wall simultaneously at, above, or below the water surface.

- When touching the wall, the hands must be separated.

- After contact with the wall is made, swimmers may turn in any manner desired.

- The shoulders must be at or past the vertical, toward the chest, when departing the wall.

- Swimmers release the hands from the wall one at a time.

- The first-hand releases from the wall by driving the elbow forcefully backward toward the opposite end of the pool.

- The arm that releases first is known as the "turning arm".

- As the elbow drives backward, the knees drive forcefully forward toward the wall.

- As the knees drive forward, the hips twist to the side, and the feet plant shoulder width apart on the wall.

- If the left-hand releases from the wall first, the hips rotate to the left and vise verse.

- The second-hand releases from the wall shortly after the first traveling behind the head into streamline.

- For speed purposes, the second-hand remains close to the surface upon releasing from the wall.

- As the second-hand releases, swimmers drop down below the surface and push off the wall.

- Swimmers should be as compact as possible during this phase of the turn.

- The speed of the elbow drive, knee tuck, hip twist, and drop down are keys to a fast turn.

- Unfortunately, many swimmers lack the core strength to perform fast tucking, twisting, and dropping actions.

- Swimmers should add core strength exercises to their dry-land training routine.

- The strength of the legs also plays an enormous role in the speed of a butterfly turn.

- To improve strength, swimmers should include plyometrics to their dry-land training routine.

- Plyometrics involves a series of explosive jumping movements using only body weight.

- Swimmers should push off the wall on the side in a 100% streamline position, with one shoulder above the other and one hip above the other, then gradually rotate fully to the chest.

- Swimmers are permitted to remain completely submerged for a distance of no more than 15-meters off a butterfly turn. By that point, the head must break the surface.

- Most age group swimmers travel less than half that distance.

- The direction of the push off can make or break a butterfly turn.

- All too often, swimmers push downward off the wall rather than outward increasing the travel time underwater and the time it takes to reach the surface.

- Most swimmers of any age should push directly out from the wall.

- Swimmers should execute the butterfly underwater travel sequence, upon pushing off the wall, consisting of a streamline phase, a body whip phase, and a breakout phase.

- The head should never lift out of streamline during the entire underwater travel sequence.

- A minimum of three body whips (butterfly kicks) should be performed off a butterfly turn, and swimmers who excel at body whip should do more.

- Body whip can be faster than swimming butterfly over a short distance.

- Swimmers should add a butterfly pull to speed up the breakout.

- Pulling to the surface puts swimmers into the flow of butterfly.

- Swimmers must be entirely on the chest before pulling or risk disqualification.

- Ideally, the body should be on the surface and fully horizontal at the completion of the butterfly pull.

- Swimmers should transition seamlessly from the underwater portion of the turn to the swimming portion.

- No breath should be taken on the first stroke off the turn to ensure a smooth transition.

BACKSTROKE TURN — INTRODUCTION

The backstroke turn is the second fastest part of a backstroke race. Unfortunately, the majority of age group swimmers have inferior backstroke turns. A backstroke turn should seem like an extension of the swim. In other words, the swim should flow smoothly into the turn, and the turn should flow smoothly into the swim. Ideally, swimmers should be able to perform a legal backstroke turn within the first year of joining a swim team, and the coach should provide extra help for those who struggle. An excellent backstroke turn is a prerequisite for college swimming.

BACKSTROKE TURN — HIGHLIGHTS

- The backstroke turn is tricky as swimmers cannot see the wall.

- Rather than look for the wall, swimmers must rely upon their stroke count.

- The stroke count represents the number of strokes from the backstroke flags to the wall.

- The first arm to enter the water as the eyes pass directly underneath the backstroke flags is stroke one.

- The stroke count for a backstroke turn is one less stroke than that used for a backstroke finish.

- A swimmer with a stroke count of six to the wall would have a stroke count of five for the turn. Eliminating one stroke provides correct space to execute a forward somersault.

- Swimmers must have complete trust in their stroke count otherwise they decelerate as they approach the wall.

- When approaching the wall, there should be no gap between the final stroke and the turn.

- The majority of age group swimmers have a gap due to a lack of knowledge and experience on how to plan for the wall.

- The gap between the last stroke and the wall causes swimmers to decelerate into the wall.

- Another common error involves getting too close to the wall on the final stroke which causes a momentary pause on the wall.

- The speed swimmers maintain into the wall determines the overall speed of the turn.

- The average speed of a practice turn is far below the speed of a competition turn.

- The majority of age group swimmers perform backstroke turns far below race pace in practice which can throw off the stroke count.

- The more often swimmers have the opportunity to race pace turns in practice, the greater the confidence and proficiency in competition.

- Swimmers are only required to touch the wall with their feet when performing a backstroke turn, and a hand touch is not necessary.

- Prior to the wall, the last arm or "turning arm" throws forcibly and diagonally over the swimmer's opposite shoulder to initiate the turn.

- As the "turning arm" throws, the body rotates from the back to the stomach with the other arm positioned against the side of the body.

- At this point, the "turning arm" is positioned forward of the shoulder.

- From here, the "turning arm" pulls back, the chin tucks into the chest, and a forward somersault is performed.

- The somersault must be as compact as possible with only the feet visible.

- Upon completion of the forward somersault, the feet plant

on the wall shoulder width, perpendicular to the surface, with the body in a face-up position.

- Ideally, the knees should achieve a 90-degree bend on the wall to ensure a powerful push off.

- The arms must reach a streamline position as the body somersaults in preparation for the push off.

- A fully streamlined upper body combined with a 90-degree knee bend creates the ideal push off position.

- From here, the legs drive off the wall.

- The strength of the legs plays an enormous role in the speed of a backstroke turn.

- To improve strength, swimmers should include plyometrics to their dry-land training routine.

- Plyometrics involves a series of explosive jumping movements using only body weight.

- Once the ideal push off position is achieved on the wall, swimmers push off the wall on the back or slightly on the side in a 100% streamline position.

- Swimmers are permitted to remain completely submerged for a distance of no more than 15-meters off a backstroke turn. By that point, the head must break the surface.

- Most age group swimmers travel less than half that distance.

- The direction of the push off can make or break a backstroke turn.

- All too often, swimmers push downward off the wall rather than outward, increasing the travel time spent underwater and the time it takes to reach the surface.

- Most swimmers of any age should push directly out from the wall.

- Swimmers should execute the backstroke underwater travel sequence, upon pushing off the wall, consisting of a streamline phase, a body whip phase, and a breakout phase.

- The head should never lift out of streamline during the entire underwater travel sequence.

- A minimum of three body whips (butterfly kicks) should be performed off a backstroke turn, and swimmers who excel at body whip should do more.

- Swimmers are not disqualified should they choose not to perform body whip off a backstroke turn.

- Body whip can be faster than backstroke over a short distance.

- Swimmers should add a backstroke pull combined with backstroke kick to speed up the breakout.

- Pulling to the surface puts swimmers into the flow of backstroke.

- Ideally, the body should be on the surface and fully horizontal at the completion of the backstroke pull.

- Swimmers should transition seamlessly from the underwater portion of the turn to the swimming portion.

BREASTSTROKE TURN — INTRODUCTION

The breaststroke turn is the second fastest part of a breaststroke race. Unfortunately, the majority of age group swimmers have inferior breaststroke turns. A breaststroke turn should seem like an extension of the swim. In other words, the swim should flow smoothly into the turn, and the turn should flow smoothly into the swim. Ideally, swimmers should be able to perform a legal breaststroke turn within the first year of joining a swim team, and the coach should provide extra help to those who struggle. An excellent breaststroke turn is a prerequisite for college swimming.

- Swimmers should begin planning the breaststroke turn at the flags and not at the wall as waiting until then leaves no time for last minute adjustments.

- When approaching the wall, there should be no gap between the final stroke and the turn.

- The majority of age group swimmers have a gap due to a lack of knowledge and experience on how to plan for the wall.

- The gap between the last stroke and the wall causes swimmers to decelerate into the wall.

- Ideally, the hands should touch the wall at the completion of the final kick to the wall.

- Another common error involves getting too close to the wall on the final stroke. This result in a momentary pause on the wall.

- The speed swimmers maintain into the wall determines the overall speed of the turn.

- The average speed of a practice turn is far below that of a competition turn.

- Swimmers who do not perform fast turns in practice are disadvantaged in competition.

- The more often swimmers have the opportunity to practice race pace turns in practice, the greater the confidence and proficiency level in competition.

- Swimmers must touch the wall entirely on the chest.

- Both hands must touch the wall simultaneously at, above, or below the water surface.

- When touching the wall, the hands must be separated.

- After contact with the wall is made, swimmers may turn in any manner desired.

- The shoulders must be at or past the vertical, toward the chest, when departing the wall.

- Swimmers release the hands from the wall one at a time.

- The first-hand releases from the wall by driving the elbow forcefully backward toward the opposite end of the pool.

- The arm that releases first is known as the "turning arm".

- As the elbow drives backward, the knees drive forcefully forward toward the wall.

- As the knees drive forward, the hips twist to the side, and the feet plant shoulder width apart on the wall.

- If the left-hand releases from the wall first, the hips rotate to the left and vise verse.

- The second-hand releases from the wall shortly after the first traveling behind the head into streamline.

- For speed purposes, the second-hand remains close to the surface upon releasing from the wall.

- As the second-hand releases, swimmers drop down below the surface and push off the wall.

- Swimmers should be as compact as possible during this phase of the turn.

- The speed of the elbow drive, knee tuck, hip twist, and drop down are keys to a fast turn.

- Unfortunately, many swimmers lack the core strength to perform fast tucking, twisting, and dropping actions.

- Swimmers should add core strength exercises to their dry-land training routine.

- The strength of the legs also plays an enormous role in the speed of a breaststroke turn.

- To improve strength, swimmers should include plyometrics to their dry-land training routine.

- Plyometrics involves a series of explosive jumping movements using only body weight.

- Swimmers should push off the wall on the side in a 100% streamline position, with one shoulder above the other and one hip above the other, then gradually rotate fully to the chest.

- Unlike the butterfly, backstroke, and the freestyle turn, there is no restriction as to how far swimmers are allowed to travel off a breaststroke turn.

- Most age group swimmers travel between five and ten yards and should surface within three to five seconds.

- The direction of the push off can make or break a breaststroke turn.

- All too often, swimmers push downward off the wall rather

than outward increasing the travel time underwater and the time it takes to reach the surface.

- Most swimmers of any age should push directly out from the wall.

- Swimmers should execute the breaststroke underwater travel sequence, upon pushing off the wall, consisting of a streamline phase, a pulldown phase, and a kick-up phase.

- To avoid disqualification, the pulldown phase cannot be initiated until the swimmer is flat on the chest.

- The head should never lift out of streamline during the entire underwater travel sequence.

- On the streamline phase, swimmers maintain a 100% streamline position and hold for one-second to take advantage of the momentum gained from pushing off the wall.

- On the pulldown phase, swimmers pull the arms down to the sides of the body pressing the palms on the thighs.

- Upon reaching the sides of the body, the arms move quickly forward to initiate the kick-up phase.

- Pausing the hands at the sides of the body causes a loss of momentum.

- Advanced-age group swimmers draw the shoulders together at the completion of the pulldown phase to further reduce drag.

- Ideally, swimmers should begin angling upward toward the surface during the pulldown phase.

- The pulling pattern used in the pulldown resembles a narrow butterfly pull as a wide pull increases drag.

- Swimmers may execute a butterfly kick at any point during the pulldown phase.

- The butterfly kick is optional, but can add additional speed.

- On the kick-up phase, swimmers draw the arms forward under the body into a streamline position.

- As the arms slide forward, the heels rise to the butt.

- A breaststroke kick is performed once the heels reach the height of the butt.

- The kick should be narrow to reduce drag.

- Ideally, the top of the head should break the surface upon the completion of the kick-up phase.

- No gap should exist between the end of the kick-up and the first above water stroke.

- Ideally, the body should be on the surface and fully horizontal at the end of the kick-up phase.

- Swimmers should transition seamlessly from the underwater portion of the turn to the swimming portion.

The freestyle turn is the second fastest part of a freestyle race. Unfortunately, the majority of age group swimmers have inferior freestyle turns. There are two types of freestyle turns. In one, a forward somersault is performed at the wall combined with a back-to-stomach streamlined push off. In the other, a forward somersault together with a twist to the side is completed at the wall combined with a side-to-stomach streamlined push off. For the sake of expediency, the forward somersault with a back-to-stomach streamlined push off is outlined here. A freestyle turn should seem like an extension of the swim. In other words, the swim should flow smoothly into the turn, and the turn should flow smoothly into the swim. Ideally, swimmers should be able to perform a legal freestyle turn within the first year of joining a swim team, and the coach should provide extra help to those who struggle. An excellent freestyle turn is a prerequisite for college swimming.

FREESTYLE TURN — HIGHLIGHTS

- Swimmers should begin planning the freestyle turn at the backstroke flags and not at the wall as waiting until the wall leaves no time for last minute adjustments.

- When approaching the wall, there should be no gap between the final stroke and the turn.

- The majority of age group swimmers have a gap due to a lack of knowledge and experience on how to plan for the wall.

- The gap between the last stroke and the wall causes swimmers to decelerate into the wall.

- Another common error involves getting too close to the wall on the final stroke which causes a momentary pause on the wall.

- The speed swimmers maintain into the wall determines the overall speed of the turn.

- The average speed of a practice turn is far below the speed of a competition turn.

- Swimmers who do not perform fast turns in practice are disadvantaged in competition.

- The more often swimmers have the opportunity to practice race pace turns in practice, the greater the confidence and proficiency level in competition.

- Swimmers are only required to touch the wall with their feet when performing a freestyle turn, and a hand touch is not necessary.

- On the final stroke to the wall, the last arm or "turning arm" is positioned forward of the shoulder with the other arm positioned against the side of the body.

- From here, the "turning arm" pulls back, the chin tucks into the chest, and a forward somersault is performed.

- The somersault must be as compact as possible with only the feet visible.

- Upon completion of the forward somersault, the feet plant on the wall shoulder width, perpendicular to the surface, with the body in a face-up position.

- Ideally, the knees should achieve a 90-degree bend on the wall to ensure a powerful push off.

- The arms must reach a streamline position as the body somersaults in preparation for the push off.

- A fully streamlined upper body combined with a 90-degree knee bend creates the ideal push off position.

- From here, the legs drive off the wall.

- The strength of the legs plays an enormous role in the speed of a freestyle turn.

- To improve strength, swimmers should include plyometrics to their dry-land training routine.

- Plyometrics involves a series of explosive jumping movements using only body weight.

- Once the ideal push off position is achieved on the wall, swimmers push off the wall on the back in a 100% streamline position gradually rotating to the stomach prior to the breakout.

- Swimmers are permitted to remain completely submerged for a distance of no more than 15-meters off a freestyle turn. By that point, the head must break the surface.

- Most age group swimmers travel less than half that distance.

- The direction of the push can make or break a freestyle turn.

- All too often, swimmers push downward off the wall rather than outward, increasing the travel time spent underwater and the time it takes to reach the surface.

- Most swimmers of any age should push directly out from the wall.

- Swimmers should execute the freestyle underwater travel sequence, upon pushing off the wall, consisting of a streamline phase, a body whip phase, and a breakout phase.

- The head should never lift out of streamline during the entire underwater travel sequence.

- A minimum of three body whips (butterfly kicks) should be performed off a freestyle turn, and swimmers who excel at body whip should do more.

- Swimmers are not disqualified should they choose not to perform body whip off a freestyle turn.

- Body whip can be faster than freestyle over a short distance.

- Swimmers should add a freestyle pull combined with freestyle kick to speed up the breakout.

- Pulling to the surface puts swimmers into the flow of freestyle.

- Ideally, the body should be on the surface and fully horizontal at the completion of the freestyle pull.

- Swimmers should transition seamlessly from the underwater portion of the turn to the swimming portion.

- No breath should be taken on the first stroke off the turn to ensure a smooth transition.

CHAPTER 5.

PHYSICAL MATTERS

LEAN MEAN SWIMMING MACHINE

To watch elite-level swimmers in action is an absolute joy. Each stroke is one of proficiency and grace. The term, "lean, mean, swimming machine" describes them perfectly. Lean suggests an efficiently fit body slipping through the water with minimum drag. Mean suggest a focused, tough, and unrelenting mind. Machine suggest flawless technique and execution. Developing swimmers with this image in mind is the absolute best way to maximize swimming potential and achieve peak performance.

GROWTH AND DEVELOPMENT

The speed of human growth is startling. At birth, infants are about one-quarter of their adult height, and they reach full height at approximately 20 years of age. Changes in the size and shape of the body occur at different times and can have a significant impact on skill acquisition. For example, at the beginning of puberty arm and leg length increase significantly and, as a result, a temporary loss of coordination is experienced. Peak growth periods generally begin at 12 years of age for girls and 14 years of age for boys although it differs from child to child. Because children develop at different times, early success in swimming may be partially or entirely due to their size and strength relative to the competition. However, success due to early maturation can be short-lived. As other swimmers hit their peak growth spurt, early maturers can be left behind. A balanced approach of mental, technical, and physical conditioning is the best way to ensure swimming success regardless of physical size.

HEIGHT IN SWIMMING

Many swimmers believe that shorter swimmers cannot be as fast as taller swimmers, but I have evidence to disprove that belief. Kiosk Hagino of Japan, medalled in all six individual events in the 2014 Asian Games earning three gold medals. He is only five-foot, eight-inches tall. Another excellent swimmer, Katinka Hosszu of Hungary, is just five-foot, six-inches tall and achieved ten victories in the 2013-1014 Arena Grand Prix Series. Both swimmers are considered short in the elite swimming world. While being short may have some disadvantages, they can be overcome through hard work and improvements in mental, technical, and physical fitness.

THE LONGER THE RACE, THE LESS SIZE MATTERS

If I had a son or daughter in swimming, I would encourage them to race distances 200-yards/meters and up. My reason is based on the role that size plays in sprint events. It is not uncommon for bigger swimmers, who are less physically and technically prepared, to beat smaller swimmers, who are more physically and technically prepared, due to a longer reach and greater strength. Distances of 200-yards/meters and up can level the playing field allowing smaller swimmers to gain the upper hand through superior technical and physical preparation.

FYI: The average height of elite-level female 50-freestylers is 5-foot,11-inches. The average height of elite-level male 50-freestylers is 6-foot, 5-inches.

NUMBER OF WEEKLY PRACTICES

Swimmers are individuals and, therefore, respond differently to training. Some thrive on six practices per week while others, of the same age and ability, struggle with four. Determining the ideal number of practices depends on a number of factors including swimmers' ability to adapt to the training stimulus. Those who appear challenged, but not overly, should remain with the current level of training while those who are sincerely struggling may be over their heads. Pushing swimmers too far beyond their current physical capacity can bring about undesirable consequences, including high levels of fatigue, injury, a decline in stroke quality, a drop in performance, and a loss of motivation. There is no advantage to giving swimmers more training than they can successfully handle.

Most team structures require that swimmers attend all designated practices. For example, if the "Silver Group" practices five times a week, every swimmer in that group is expected to attend that number of practices. A good coach will monitor swimmers to ensure that the training stimulus is appropriate and make adjustments where needed. If adjustments are not made, parents should arrange a meeting with the coach to discuss their concerns respectfully. Should the issue persist, parents would be wise to allow their child to miss an occasional practice. Though many coaches disapprove of this practice, some children need additional time to adapt. In my view, one size does not fit all and one practice regime does not fit all.

The amount of weekly practices offered differs from team to team. As a general rule, swimmers who compete at the local level should attend three to four practices a week. State-level swimmers should attend at least four to six practices a week. National-level swimmers should attend at least six to eight practices a week. International-level swimmers participate in eight or more practices a week.

Parents must keep in mind that the career of a committed swimmer can last 10, 15, or even 20 years. An excessive number of practices early on can have a detrimental effect over the long term. Finishing strong is more important than starting strong.

TRADITIONAL VERSUS CONTEMPORARY

I recognize that swim parents are not swim coaches and that 99.9% of them have no desire to coach swimming. But I also believe that parents should have some understanding of the type of training their child is subjected to as the method used will undoubtedly impact their child's level of success. Currently, there are two basics schools of thought regarding swim training. One is a traditional model that has been in existence for many, many decades. The other is a more contemporary model circa 1980's.

The traditional model promotes a disproportionate amount of aerobic conditioning performed well below swimmers' maximum speed. The theory is based on the belief that swimmers must develop a broad aerobic base in order to be competitive now and in the future. Practices tend to be higher in yardage and lower in speed. Many of the top coaches in the USA and abroad adhere to this model.

The contemporary model places a far greater emphasis on anaerobic conditioning as well as race specific training. Fewer coaches subscribe to this model, but its popularity is quickly growing. Michael Andrews, the current age group superstar, is trained using the contemporary model. Practices tend to be lower in yardage and higher in speed. I happen to believe that the contemporary model is more practical, productive, and delivers the best results to a broader cross-section of swimmers.

YARDAGE ALONE IS NOT THE ANSWER

Many swimmers who attend my camps train a minimum of eleven months a year and attend a minimum of seven practices per week. On average, they swim 6,000 yards a practice for a rough total of 1,848,000 yards per year! One would think with that amount of yardage, swimmers would find it easy to achieve best times and their swimming goals. Unfortunately, quantity without quality, can only take swimmers so far. To achieve more, swimmers must place equal importance on the development of superior start, stroke, and turn technique.

SWIMMING SMARTER IS HARDER

Improving physical fitness is typically the primary focus of swim practice. Training sets of ever-increasing yardage, on faster and faster intervals, is the standard protocol used to achieve this objective. While effective, combining technical demands with physical demands is even more effective. For example, it is much harder to maintain maximum distance per stroke, a high elbow catch, and a continuous kick throughout a training set than just focusing on physical output. Emphasizing the technical side, as well as the physical, takes fitness to a higher level. Parents should seek out swim teams that emphasize both.

PHYSICAL FITNESS HELPS TECHNICAL FITNESS

To develop proper start, stroke, and turn technique, swimmers require a certain degree of strength, flexibility, and endurance. For example, strength is required to perform a high elbow catch in freestyle, flexibility is required to perform a chest press in butterfly, and endurance is required to maintain a six-beat kick in freestyle. Without question, proper technique and physical fitness go hand in hand.

OVER PREPARE TO OVERACHIEVE

The ability to perform at peak levels is related to how well swimmers prepare beforehand. Over-prepared swimmers exude confidence, perform at higher skill levels, and achieve better results. Under-prepared swimmers exhibit doubt, make numerous technical and tactical errors, and struggle at best. To ensure peak performance swimmers must ramp up their preparation weeks or months before competing. Using a hypothetical scale from one-to-ten, if the perceived level of challenge for an upcoming mid-season swim meet rates an eight, swimmers must put forth a constant "nine effort" in practice. Alternatively, if the perceived level of challenge for an upcoming championship swim meet rates a ten, they must put forth an "eleven effort", figuratively speaking of course. Performing at peak levels is no accident, but rather the result of timely and progressive preparation.

THE FATIGUE FACTOR

Fatigue effects stroke and turn quality. At the onset of fatigue strokes shorten and turns lose their snap. To maintain stroke and turn quality over the course of a race, swimmers must have the physical fitness that can last the distance of the race. Technical skills without physical fitness is a losing course of action.

SWIMMING STRENGTH

When it comes to body strength, swimmers fall into one of the three general categories, those who are stronger or weaker than their physical size, and those who fit somewhere in the middle. Physical size or mass equates to drag in the water and the greater the size or mass, the greater the drag. While swimmers have little control over their physical size or mass, they can alter their strength and gain the upper hand. To build the necessary strength, swimmers should participate in a well-executed dry-land training program at least three to five times per week. At one time, dry-land training was more of an afterthought. Today, it is essential.

Contrary to popular belief, strength training is not inappropriate or harmful to young swimmers provided the dry-land training program is scientifically sound and executed with safety in mind. This position is well-documented and supported by the American Academy of Pediatrics (APP). Other organizations that support this view include the American College of Sports Medicine (ACSM), the American Orthopedic Society for Sports Medicine (AOSSM), and the National Strength and Conditioning Association (NSCA).

KICKING IS KEY

At many times, I have felt like a lonely voice in the wilderness, promoting an idea that very few coaches or swimmers agree with. Case in point: I have always believed that swimmers should maintain a six-beat kick (six kicks per two strokes) when swimming freestyle even though the upper body is the primary source of swimming propulsion. Coaches have vehemently opposed me and swimmers have considered me crazy. In spite of their reactions, I continue to believe that six-beat kicking is the way to go, due to the many inherent benefits. These include enhanced body position, stability, balance, timing, rotation, improved stroke efficiency, propulsion, and a greater balance of work between the arms and the legs.

While surfing the web one day I came across an article written by Russell Mark, the current High-Performance Consultant for United States Swimming. In the article, he cites that all six medalists in the distance events at 2012 Olympics used a six-beat kick. Finally, I feel redeemed!

SHOULDER INJURIES IN SWIMMING

Competitive swimmers perform ten times the number of movements of other overhand athletes putting the shoulders at greater risk of severe harm. They also have a 70 percent chance of developing a shoulder related injury sometime during their careers.

Optimal shoulder function in swimmers relies upon the musculature of the rotator cuff, shoulder blades, lower back, and abdominals plus ligaments in the shoulder. Imbalances or damage can occur within any of these areas due to poor swimming technique.

Russell Mark, the High-Performance Consultant for United States Swimming, states: "It is not necessarily repeated strokes that cause shoulder pain. It is repeated strokes with flawed technique."

It does not take a significant flaw to cause a serious problem. If a swimmer swam 3,000 yards or meters in practice, which is not uncommon and averaged 18 strokes per length, it would equal 2,160 strokes! Even with a small flaw, the number of repetitions could easily result in a shoulder injury. The flawed technique in the butterfly, backstroke, and breaststroke can also contribute to injury.

A 2010 study of 80 elite Australian swimmers (age 13-26) and published in the British Journal of Medicine found that 91% experienced shoulder pain due to flawed technique or overuse!

Most swimming parents are aware that their child suffers from faulty technique, but either ignore the problem hoping it fixes itself or do not know how best to address it. Ignoring the problem is not the solution as it puts the child at a greater risk of injury. Solving the problem via sound stroke development is an essential part of shoulder health and prolonged swimming success.

SLEEP MATTERS

There are numerous ways to enhance swimming performance including sleep. Stanford researcher, Cheri D. Mah, found that when male basketball players slept ten hours a night performance in practice dramatically improved. Free-throw and three-point shooting increased by an average of nine percent. Daytime naps had a similar effect on performance. When night air traffic controllers took naps of 40 minutes and slept an average of 19 minutes, they performed much better on tests that measured vigilance and reaction time. To achieve peak performance swimmers must view sleep and rest as essential parts of the training regime. Restoring one's body is basic human physiology.

FLEXIBILITY MATTERS

Flexibility plays a crucial role in speed production in swimming. "Decrease your stiffness to improve your swiftness" is an expression I often use to convey its vital importance. To understand the role that flexibility plays envision a cheetah in pursuit of its prey or a racehorse at full speed.

Some coaches place a high importance on stretching and include stretching as part of daily training while others feel that it is a waste of time. Regardless of the view, these facts are irrefutable:

- Stretching increases the length of muscle fibers, and longer muscle fibers generate more force when contracted.

- Stretching assists in the correct posture by lengthening tight muscles that pull areas of the body away from their intended positions.

- Stretching improves range of motion and muscle coordination.

- Stretching enhances blood flow and nutrient supply.

- Stretching prevents injury.

YOGA FOR SWIMMERS

Yoga found its way into the Peak Performance Swim Camp curriculum in 2005. That was the year I began taking yoga at a local studio. Among the many things that surprised me was the correlation between specific yoga poses and specific competitive swimming postures. It occurred to me that if swimmers had the opportunity to perform select yoga poses on land, it would be much easier for them to perform the relative swimming postures in the water. For example, performing the yoga pose Downward Dog significantly improves swimmers' understanding of the all-important chest-pressing action in the butterfly. Frequent repetition of the pose also develops the essential physical qualities (flexibility and strength) necessary to perform the posture repeatedly when swimming. Other examples include the Cobra Pose for the breaststroke breathing action, the Bridge Pose for the backstroke start, the Yoga Plank Pose for freestyle body position, and the Warrior 3 Pose for streamlining. Other yoga benefits include improved joint mobility, enhanced strength, injury prevention, and heightened muscle recovery.

HYPERVENTILATION DANGER

Hyperventilation is breathing that is deeper and more rapid than normal. Swimmers often postpone the need to breathe by hyperventilating before diving off a starting block or pushing off a wall, but this can have very dangerous consequences. Hyperventilation decreases the immediate need to breathe which lowers the amount of oxygen in the blood. If oxygen levels become too low, swimmers can lose consciousness. Hyperventilation can be voluntary or involuntary, but either can have an adverse outcome. While breath holding is a common practice in swimming, swimmers should be vigilant and breathe whenever the urge to breathe is high. Parents should discuss the dangers of hyperventilation with their child.

EXCESSIVE COUGHING IN PRACTICE

If swimmers cough excessively during practice, it may be the result of chloramines, a combination of chlorine and ammonia. Chloramines form when chlorine mixes with proteins like shredded skin and hair. The more chlorine and protein in the water the more chloramines. This toxic byproduct tends to settle on the surface of the water, where swimmers breathe. Research indicates that these coughing bouts are of little risk to healthy young swimmers. To be on the safe side parents should speak to the coach if their child coughs persistently at practice.

SWIMMER'S EAR

Swimmer's ear is an infection of the ear canal caused by contaminated water or debris (wax or dead skin) in the ear canal which harbors germs. It is very prevalent in younger swimmers due to a narrow ear canal. My best advice is to see a doctor to ensure that there is no debris in the ear. If the debris remains, the infection will most likely linger. Custom-made earplugs can help in reducing ear infections.

NUTRITION AND SWIMMING

Proper nutrition is critical to meeting the demands of swim training. Falling behind nutritionally, even for a few days, can seriously undermine swimmers' ability to perform at peak levels. It is not uncommon for swimmers to blame a poor practice or performance on fatigue, when, in fact, it was caused by poor nutrition.

Swimmers should aim for a well-balanced diet with a variety of carbohydrates, lean proteins, and healthful fats. They should consume fresh fruit and vegetables (versus high processed varieties) and avoid soda, candy, and fast food. Carbohydrates should be the main focus of meals, but protein is also important.

Swim meets also present a nutritional challenge. Although most swimming events are relatively brief, swimming multiple events over multiple days can seriously deplete hydration and glucose levels thus impeding performance.

Fluid loss is one of the greatest threats to peak performance. High-intensity practices, heated pools, exposure to hot temperatures, and high humidity lead to significant losses of fluid and sodium via sweat. Marathon swim meets can also result in fluid loss. Many swimmers gauge fluid loss based on how thirsty they feel at the moment, but the sensation of thirst does not take effect until after a significant loss of fluid has occurred. To ensure adequate hydration levels, swimmers should consume 14-20 ounces of water prior to the start of the day. Current hydration levels can be determined by observing urine color. Urine, light in color, indicates good hydration, while urine, the color of apple juice, indicates poor hydration. Swimmers should rehydrate periodically throughout the training session or competition.

Consuming energy gels at the same time can help to refuel glycogen levels. Most gels are designed to be consumed every 20-45 minutes.

NUTRITION AND MORNING PRACTICE

Many swimmers arrive at morning practice on an empty stomach, with glycogen levels low due to overnight fasting. These high-carb options are an excellent way to start the day:

- Toast, jam, and fruit juice.

- Fruit smoothie with mango, banana, berries, and low-fat yogurt.

- Meal replacement drinks.

- High-carb bars, energy gels, or energy chews.

- Cold or hot cereal with fruit and low-fat or skim milk.

- French toast or pancakes with maple or fruit syrup.

- Breakfast burrito (scrambled eggs, salsa, and low-fat cheese in a whole wheat tortilla).

- Bagel or English muffin with jelly or peanut butter.

- Small roll or sandwich made with banana and honey.

NUTRITION AND RECOVERY

Contrary to popular belief, the physical benefits derived from training are not fully realized until after training has ended. It is during this period that repair to damaged muscle fibers occurs; leading to greater muscle strength and endurance. Swimmers who actively promote recovery, via sound nutritional habits, reap the rewards, while those who ignore this all-important process pay the consequences. Eating healthy sources of protein and carbohydrates immediately following practice enables sore muscles to recover quicker. The sooner swimmers consume these nutrients; the sooner the healing process begins. These recovery snack and meal options substantially improve the recovery process:

- Rolls or bagels.

- Peanut-butter-and-jelly sandwiches.

- Salted pretzels.

- Fresh fruit.

- Fruit smoothie.

- Low-fat cheese and crackers.

- Low-fat chocolate milk.

- Protein bars, protein shakes, and meal replacements.

- High-carb bars, energy gels, and energy chews.

On the day of competition, a high-carb meal should be consumed at least two hours prior to competing. Swimmers should avoid slow-to-digest high-fat foods such as bacon, sausage, cheese omelets, and fried potatoes. To ensure adequate hydration 14-20 oz of water or a sports drink should be consumed prior to the start of the day. Swimmers should also monitor their urine color throughout the day to ensure ideal hydration levels. The darker the urine, the greater need for hydration. Energy levels should be maintained throughout competition via water or sports drinks, fresh fruit, sandwiches, cereal, granola bars, high-carb bars, energy gels, or energy chews. Swimmers should also remember to jump-start the recovery process once the competition is over for the day by consuming additional protein for muscle repair, carbs to reload glycogen levels, and fluids for rehydration.

VEGETARIAN SWIMMERS

A vegetarian diet for swimmers is not that different from a normal healthy diet with the exception of meat. The biggest challenge in a vegetarian diet is consuming enough protein. Eating a wide variety of foods that include some protein at each meal can ensure that swimmers get their daily requirement. Protein food sources include beans, chickpeas, black beans, and pinto beans. Other sources include eggs, soy products, cheese, cottage cheese, protein powder, tofu, and tempeh. When choosing nuts, pistachios are an excellent option as they are lower in fat than other nuts.

Vitamin B12, traditionally found only in meat, is an essential vitamin for swimmers. Fortunately, many cereals and soy milk products are now fortified with B12.

Drinking pure fruit juice is a great way to ensure vegetarian swimmers get sufficient amounts of calories, as they have plenty of calories and healthful benefits.

STARCHY CARBS

Despite the media spin that all carbs are bad, starchy carbs are an excellent fuel source for swimmers. Sweet potatoes contain simple starches and are rich in complex carbohydrates. full of fiber, and Vitamin A. Avoid adding brown sugar to this super food. Beans and lentils occupy two spaces on the U.S.D.A. Food Guide Pyramid, and are excellent sources of carbs, protein, fiber, potassium, and iron. Pasta is a favorite among swimmers. For added nutritional benefits, choose whole grain over durum wheat flour. The lowly potato is an excellent carb food and high in fiber, potassium, Vitamin B6, and Vitamin C. Vitamin B6 is necessary for the breakdown of glycogen and plays a key role in athletic performance. Rice is high in carbs and low in fat. Choosing brown rice or wild rice will add extra fiber and other health benefits. Quinoa is considered by most to be a grain, but in fact it is a seed. It is a high source of carbs, protein, fiber, potassium, healthy fats, and magnesium. Corn gets a bad rap, but it is a great source of carbs and contains protein, iron, B6, and magnesium. Peas add variety to a diet and provides carbs as well as potassium, fiber, protein, and Vitamin C.

IRON DEFICIENCY

Due to high rates of exertion, swimmers can easily become overly fatigued. Lack of sleep, stress, illness, and nutritional imbalances can worsen the problem. Among nutritional imbalances, a lack of essential iron in the blood is most typical. Iron plays a major role in swimming performance as it assists in the transport of oxygen through the blood stream. A lack of iron can lead to decreased performance, sleepiness and undue fatigue, poor concentration, moodiness or irritability, and decreased immune function. It is possible to improve iron stores through a well structured eating plan. Iron-rich foods include beef, chicken, shrimp, oysters, and fish. Brussels sprouts, broccoli, tomatoes, potatoes, and green and red peppers can improve the absorption rate of iron. Vegetarians must ensure that they get adequate amounts of Vitamin B 12 in their diets. Parents should consider a blood test if they feel their child is iron deficient.

Made in the USA
Columbia, SC
13'October 2021

46969985R00068